Puppies

Complete Care Made Easy

Puppies

A Guide to Caring for Your Puppy

By Amy Fernandez

Photographs by Isabelle Francais

BOWTIE PRESS®

Irvine, California

Karla Austin, *Business Operations Manager*
Nick Clemente, *Special Consultant*
Barbara Kimmel, *Managing Editor*
Jarelle Stein, *Editor*
Jackie Franza, *Consulting Editor*
Honey Winters, *Design*
Indexed by Melody Englund

The puppies in this book are referred to as *he* and *she* in alternating chapters unless their gender is apparent from the activity discussed.

Library of Congress Cataloging-in-Publication Data

Fernandez, Amy.
 Puppies : a guide to caring for your puppy / Amy Fernandez ; photographs by Isabelle Francais.
    p. cm. — (Complete care made easy)
  Includes index.
  ISBN 1-931993-76-9
 1. Puppies. I. Title. II. Series.

  SF427.F462 2006
  636.7'07—dc22
                        2006002178

BowTie Press®
A Division of BowTie, Inc.
3 Burroughs
Irvine, California 92618

Printed and bound in Singapore
Second Printing in 2007:
10 09 08 07   2 3 4 5 6 7 8 9 10

Acknowledgments

DEDICATED TO MY FRIEND BRENDA MACON, THE BEST owner any puppy could hope for. My thanks to Barbara Kimmel, who helped to shape this book.

—Amy Fernandez

Contents

1

All About Puppies

A new owner cuddles her pug puppy.

ACCORDING TO THE 2005/2006 AMERICAN PET Products Manufacturers Association's National Pet Ownership Survey, Americans own more than seventy-three million dogs. There are many reasons for owning a dog, among them are the sheer fun and unconditional love a dog offers. For many people, no aspect of dog ownership is more rewarding than the bonding, nurturing, and trust that come from raising a puppy. It is a remarkable experience on many levels. Regardless of how hectic or demanding your life is, the day-to-day responsibilities of caring for a puppy keep you grounded and remind you to appreciate what is really important in life—your relationships with the people and animals around you. In addition, modern science has proven that daily interaction with a dog is just plain good for you! Studies have shown that owning a dog lowers stress, encourages regular daily exercise, and often speeds recovery times after major surgery.

Puppies Through the Ages

People have recognized and enjoyed the benefits of canine companionship for thousands of years. Many historians believe this enduring bond began when ancient humans adopted and raised orphaned wolf puppies. Archaeological excavations have discovered wolf and human remains at the same sites dating back four hundred thousand years. The wolf was the first species to be successfully domesticated.

DNA evidence and physical variations between ancient wolf and modern-day dog skeletons show that the dog was a genetically separate species from the wolf at least forty thousand years ago and was definitely domesticated by fifteen thousand years ago. By the beginning of the Stone Age (circa 7000 BC), the dog had become a common feature of human settlements, whereas evidence of domesticated livestock did not begin to appear at human habitation sites until one thousand years later.

Researchers believe that the domestic dog first evolved in eastern Asia. The "parent" animals were descendants of a smaller wolf species, the Indian wolf. From eastern Asia, early dogs migrated with humans to populate the Middle East, Africa, and Europe and eventually across the Siberian land bridge to North and South America.

Scientists comparing ancient wolf skulls with today's dog skulls have found the latter to be smaller and more rounded, with narrower jaws, shorter muzzles, and smaller teeth. These physical changes of domestication were accompanied by equally dramatic behavioral changes. The domestication process altered the wolf's natural wariness, making the dog more trusting, curious, and tolerant of unfamiliar experiences. The ability to accept variations in diet and living conditions allowed the dog to benefit from the emerging ecological niche created by human evolution.

Domestication actually enhanced the wolf's reproductive capability. A primary feature of domestication is the ability to breed in captivity. At least eight thousand years ago, humans began deciding which animals would be bred. Canine traits originally developed in response to natural selection were suppressed or enhanced through artificial selection. So began the evolution of specialized dog breeds.

Hunting dogs were selectively bred to be larger, smaller, faster, or stronger to better pursue different types of game. As humans became increasingly dependent on livestock and farming, dogs were adapted to new roles, including herding and

The ancestors of this trio of wire fox terriers were bred by English hunters to root foxes out of their lairs and to kill vermin.

guarding valuable livestock, defending a homestead in an owner's absence, and eradicating mice and rats.

Ancient civilizations, such as those of the Greeks, Romans, Persians, and Celts, contributed to the creation of specialized dog breeds. The forerunners of most of our modern purebreds (mastiffs, greyhounds, spaniels, and terriers) existed in some form by the Middle Ages. Hunting dogs, sheepdogs, and terriers remained vital to the survival of most of the population. Certain breeds—for instance, refined sporting dogs such as the Scottish deerhound and exotic companion breeds such as the Maltese—were primarily associated with the aristocracy.

Modern purebreds trace their roots to the formation of the first dog shows and kennel clubs in the mid-nineteenth century, when breeds were defined and categorized according to ancestry and purpose. New breeds, such as the fox terrier and the Brussels griffon, were developed; exotic foreign breeds, such as the Pekingese, were brought to public attention; and many popular breeds, such as the Irish setter, transitioned from the realm of the working dog to that of the companion dog. More than four hundred recognized dog breeds exist today.

Puppies Today

Most dogs no longer fulfill their original functions, but this has not diminished their appeal. Humans still choose to share their lives with dogs of every shape and size. Their varied talents are suited to every interest and lifestyle. There are, for example, sporting breeds that make good matches for active dog owners and companion breeds better suited for a quiet life at home. Some breeds remain highly popular despite the fact that their traditional working roles have become obsolete. Conformation

Conformation Dog Shows

Purebred puppies of all breeds can compete at conformation dog shows to earn championship titles and national rankings. The American Kennel Club and the United Kennel Club are the major organizations sponsoring conformation shows in the United States, and many smaller organizations offer titles for rare and unrecognized breeds. They all provide separate classes for puppies, and many feature special competitions and prizes for puppies. Entries in each class are graded first through fourth place according to how well participants conform to the breed's Standard of Perfection, or Breed Standard. First place winners in the classes advance to the next level of competition to earn championship points. Here, they must defeat the other Best of Breed winners from that particular group and Best in Show competition, in which all of the Best in Group winners compete for the top prize. Major shows can be extremely competitive. If you are considering showing your puppy in conformation events, start by enrolling her in a conformation training class, where she'll learn the basics of how to move properly on a lead and how to stand for examination.

shows and Earthdog, field, and herding trials ensure that unique canine traits are not lost. A working trial can provide an outlet for your dog's natural instincts and give you an opportunity to appreciate her traditional heritage.

What to Expect from Your Puppy

All puppies undergo several distinct phases of development before they reach maturity. Each phase is designed to prepare them for the next one. During these phases, they learn to bond with their owners and understand their places in the human "pack," to explore new environments, and to recognize dangers.

Although these German shorthaired pointers may never be used to trail and retrieve prey as their forebears did, they still make great companions, especially for families with children.

Birth to Four Weeks (Neonatal Period)

During her first month, a puppy spends 90 percent of her time sleeping. When she is awake, she instinctively seeks food from her mother (the dam). This behavior pattern changes abruptly when the puppy reaches three weeks of age and begins interacting with the environment. Her eyes open between ten and fourteen days, and her ears begin functioning between fifteen and twenty-four days—and suddenly she becomes aware of the world around her. She learns to stand and walk, and within another week, she leaves the whelping box to explore her new surroundings.

As her first milk teeth erupt, she becomes curious to taste real food and begins weaning off mother's milk. She also starts to

Two Chinese crested puppies, just weeks old, peer down at the world from a new vantage point. Like all puppies, they are intensely curious about their surroundings

explore her environment by chewing and tasting. The puppy starts responding to humans and playing with her mother and littermates.

Four to Six Weeks (Individual Awareness Period)

By the time a puppy is four weeks old, she is displaying hints of personality. As she becomes more motivated to socialize and explore, she becomes more independent and begins experimenting with her place in the pack.

A puppy's pack can consist of not only dogs but also people. One of the earliest indications of a puppy's pack instinct is her following someone around as soon she can walk. Puppies have an innate urge to bond with others, whether it's with their littermates or with the breeder. By five weeks of age, a puppy will start demanding attention. She will respond when called and wag her tail when happy.

An exuberant young shiba inu tries to interest an older packmate in a bit of play. Puppies at this age want lots of attention

Six to Eight Weeks (Socialization and Exploration Period)

By six weeks, the puppy has a complete set of primary, or puppy, teeth, and weaning onto solid food is nearly complete. Although she no longer needs her dam for sustenance, the puppy still depends on her for training, comfort, and moral support.

Puppies at this age easily accept new experiences, so breeders generally make this the time to introduce the pups to handling and grooming. This introduction is part of *socialization*, a term dog professionals use to refer to the exposure of puppies to people, places, and experiences in an effort to prevent them from growing into fearful (sometimes aggressive) dogs. An experienced, reputable breeder starts the socialization process early, teaching her puppies about regular household noises such as blenders, vacuums, and slamming doors. Sound effect CDs can be used to introduce other new sounds, such as thunder and the cacophony of a busy city street. (See chapter 7 for more on socialization.)

Breeders normally begin training their puppies to be handled and groomed during these weeks because they easily accept new things at this age. A puppy should be introduced to important aspects of her lifestyle by eight weeks because she is mentally programmed to accept unusual and potentially startling events such as noisy vacuum cleaners, slamming screen doors, and talking parrots. If she is born and raised in a home, this happens as a matter of routine. If a kennel-raised puppy is introduced to these things at a later age, it is more challenging for her to absorb them.

Eight to Twelve Weeks (Fear Imprinting Period)

At this time, a puppy usually receives her first vaccination, which may be a single or combination vaccination, depending on what your breeder or veterinarian has recommended. Exposure to other dogs and areas frequented by dogs should be minimized until your puppy has had two vaccinations. By eight weeks, the puppy will have little or no natural immunity that was conferred by her dam at birth. Until she develops immunity from vaccinations, she remains susceptible to many communicable canine diseases. This is also when many puppies go to their new homes, and the primary social attachment is transferred from dogs to humans. The puppy will need daily social contact and lots of positive reinforcement with praise and petting in response to desirable behavior.

And you will need to maintain an upbeat attitude to reassure the puppy during potentially frightening new experiences and to ensure that she makes a smooth adjustment.

Eight- to twelve-week-old shepherd mix pups pile on top of each other for comfort and warmth.

Twelve to Sixteen Weeks (Independence Period)

The puppy normally receives her second and third vaccinations at approximately twelve and sixteen weeks, respectively. Once inoculated, she can be introduced to new people and places. Daily socialization and short training sessions will counteract fear and instill confidence and good manners. (See chapter 7 for more on socialization.)

By fourteen weeks, the spontaneous desire to socialize and investigate begins to wane, and a puppy becomes wary of unfamiliar people and places. Continually introducing her to new experiences becomes increasingly important. The lessons of socialization must be consistently reinforced until a puppy reaches adulthood—and beyond.

Fear Imprinting

THE PERIOD FROM EIGHT TO TWELVE WEEKS IS SOMETIMES referred to as the fear imprinting period because a puppy becomes more sensitive to her surroundings. As puppies investigate their new surroundings, they learn that some things should be feared. This can be something straightforward, such as physical pain, harsh correction, or bullying by other pets. Or, it can result from an irrational reaction to something unusual. A sound-sensitive puppy can become overly fearful in response to a car backfiring, fire crackers popping, or a noisy parade traipsing down Main Street. A touch-sensitive puppy can have difficulty recovering if someone accidentally steps on her foot or tail. Although fear imprinting is a temporary phase, try to minimize stress during these weeks. A few bad experiences can set a pattern that may be difficult to overcome and permanently affect a puppy's personality.

Here is a chronological breakdown of the stages related to fear imprinting:

- *Three to four weeks: puppies won't hesitate to approach anything interesting and don't generally learn from their "mistakes."*

- *Five weeks: puppies begin to develop a sense of fear, based on memory and experience, and become more cautious.*

- *Seven weeks: puppies have good memories, and fear responses can form quickly.*

- *Nine weeks: fear imprinting usually peaks.*

- *Ten weeks: unwarranted fear reactions usually level off as the puppies' understanding of their environment becomes more reliable.*

Four to Six Months (Preadolescent Period)

At four months, a puppy's permanent teeth begin to grow in, replacing her primary ones. Unlike the earlier teething phase, this one can be associated with behavior problems. A puppy may become temperamental due to the discomfort, but fortunately her moodiness will be short lived.

Social pressures will become a larger issue for the puppy as adolescence approaches. Puppies become more conscious of their positions in the household pack, attempting either to fit in or to improve their status. Adult dogs have the least tolerance for puppies of this age; what used to be a soft nip at the ear from a tiny pup becomes a rather painful bite from a puppy who has grown to almost adult size. Both humans and other dogs in the household start expecting a puppy to behave properly, like the rest of the pack. Ideally, the puppy will possess the essential social skills and stress tolerance to cope with these demands.

The Teenage Puppy (Six Months to Two Years: Adolescence)

Adolescence presents a multitude of challenges—not only for the puppy but also for the puppy owner. Owners generally expect puppies at this age to exhibit reliable house-training and adult demeanor. However, the fact that your adolescent puppy looks more like an adult dog does not automatically mean she is capable of thinking or behaving like one. In fact, her physical, emotional, and mental resources may take a nosedive.

During adolescence, even well-socialized puppies can experience some insecurity and instability. For example, some puppies may become suspicious of strangers or act uncharacteristically submissive in response to stress or reprimand. Some will become markedly more aggressive. Although training and reinforcement of desired behavior will not guarantee that adolescent behavior problems won't arise, your efforts will certainly help to minimize such

Like their human counterparts, adolescent dogs, such as this shepherd, may exhibit behavioral problems. They may become insecure and more submissive—or more aggressive.

problems. At six months of age, puppies become eligible to compete in formal dog shows and performance events, which bring structured training routines and competitive aspirations.

2
Choosing a Puppy

A litter of border collies hobnob with a lamb, who may be a future charge. Affectionate and protective, these herding dogs can be a good choice for families.

THERE ARE PLENTY OF REASONS TO WANT A PUPPY. The trick is to make sure your reasons are the right ones. It's easy to imagine how a puppy can enhance your life—as a devoted friend, a watchdog, a playmate, an exercise buddy. But owning a puppy is a two-way street. A puppy will create major changes in your lifestyle—more than just vet bills and rug cleaning. Are you prepared to cope with the added responsibility? If you decide you are ready to be an owner, you will need to determine which dog is right for you, choosing one who will fit in with your lifestyle. Different breeds have different requirements and temperaments, and it may take time to find the perfect puppy. Even after deciding on a breed, you will find that the pups in a litter all have individual personalities.

The first step, however, is to determine whether you are prepared to cope with the added responsibility of owning a puppy. Begin by asking yourself some general questions.

Does a Puppy Fit Your Lifestyle?

Do you know what it's really like to live with a dog? If your ideas about dog ownership consist mainly of childhood memories, update this with some current experience. Do more than visit dogs belonging to friends or relatives. Offer to dog sit for a week or two, and see whether you still feel enthusiastic about getting a dog (keep in mind that puppies will require more attention than adult dogs will). Or volunteer at a local animal shelter. Working with so many dogs will definitely tell you if you have the patience and stamina for a puppy.

This chow chow's paws-on approach to mealtime will mean extra cleanup work for the owner. Be sure to consider these kinds of chores when deciding whether you have time for a puppy.

Do you have time for a puppy? Abundant leisure time or a flexible schedule does not automatically mean you want to devote this precious resource to puppy care. Do you want to spend your lunch hour going home to walk or feed a puppy? Or spend your weekends at puppy training classes? Or get up an hour early every day to tend to puppy chores?

Utilizing time at doggy day care, employing a dog walking service, and taking a trip to a dog park can supplement your daily attention, but they cannot replace it. And every puppy comes with his own set of quirks and charms; you may have a collie who develops an independent spirit, or you may end up with a golden retriever who never wants to leave your side. Unless you have the time to raise a puppy, you will not be able to manage the quirks or enjoy the charms.

This French bulldog looks tuckered out after a game of Frisbee. Playing with your puppy is critical to his development.

Does everyone in your household want a puppy? It is unrealistic to assume that only one person will be responsible for a puppy's care. Everyone in your home will interact with him in some way, and the puppy will seek attention from everyone. Whoever spends the most time at home will be faced with a greater share of daily responsibilities—including dealing with messes and dog damage. This is bound to create resentment unless everyone wants a puppy.

Can you accommodate a puppy? Space requirements vary by breed and by temperament. Some big dogs are surprisingly sedate, and some very small ones are energetic. A large, fenced yard, once considered essential for a puppy, is helpful but not mandatory. Active dogs can live happily in small apartments—if you are prepared to devote the necessary time and effort to meeting their daily exercise requirements (see chapter 5).

Along with exercise needs, puppies come with lots of accessories—beds, crates, bins of dog food, pens, toys—all over the house. Do you have room for all this stuff in the middle of your kitchen, bedroom, or living room? Social interaction is critical to a puppy's development. He cannot be relegated to some inconspicuous part of the house. Similarly, is your car large enough to safely transport your dog? If you don't have a car, how will you get your puppy to the veterinary clinic and other necessary places?

Are you prepared for the financial outlay? A puppy can be more expensive than you bargained for. Dog food, for instance, will cost you $20 to $30 for a large bag; for the biggest breeds, you'll be buying at least one bag per month. Other essentials, such as beds and crates, collars and leads, treats and toys, and grooming supplies, might add $200 to $300 annually. This still sounds manageable. Add in basic veterinary care: inoculations

($100 per year), heartworm test and preventive care ($50 to $100 per year), microchip ($50 to $75), spay or neuter ($100 to $400), and dental care ($100 to $300). Puppies may also need one or more professional services on a regular basis. Consider puppy training classes ($100 to $200), doggy day care or a dog sitter ($10 to $20 per day), a professional dog walker ($10 per day), and professional grooming ($20 to $50 per visit). Other expenses can include annual dog licensing, pet health insurance, and increased premiums for homeowners insurance or pet-related security deposits on rental units.

These figures are only general guidelines. They should, however, give you a realistic idea of the financial investment you will be making. The costs certainly are not meant to dissuade you from getting a puppy, only to prepare you.

A veterinarian examines three Pomeranian puppies. Good veterinary care is a crucial on-going expense, so be prepared for it.

Finding the Puppy of Your Dreams

Once you have decided that a puppy is the pet for you, the first step in choosing a puppy is to determine the breed (or mixed breed) that you want. Research the breeds you are interested in to learn about their general temperaments and care requirements, which will help identify a breed that fits in with your lifestyle. Here are some basic guidelines and information to get you started in your research.

Which "Model" Is for You?

Dogs come in three basic "models": purebred, crossbred, and random bred. All three make wonderful pets. But none of them comes with a built-in guarantee of health, quality, or completely predictable behavior. Be wary of anyone, be it breeder or rescue group, claiming otherwise. Dogs are also classified in groups by type—such as working, hound, and sport—and by breed. The more you know about the characteristics of dogs in these classifications, the wiser you'll be in choosing your companion pup.

PUREBRED

With purebreds, both parents are documented (registered) as belonging to the same breed. Offspring are recognized as members of the same breed and are eligible for certification with the same registry. A registry is an internationally recognized organization that maintains parentage and ownership records of purebred dogs. If a dog is registered by one of these organizations, such as American Kennel Club (AKC) or the Fédération Cynologique Internationale (FCI), other official registries for that same breed automatically accept his pedigree. Purebred puppies are the product of several generations of dogs with similar mental and physical traits, such as size, personality, and health. Although these traits will still vary, the extent of variation is much more predictable.

CROSSBRED

Crossbred means both parents are certified purebreds but of different breeds. Sometimes, crossbred puppies represent the best breed qualities of both parents, but this is not always true. Crossbreeding increases unpredictability of mental and physical traits.

RANDOM BRED

Random bred puppies are also known as mixed breeds or mongrels (or mutts). Their ancestry can be estimated but not verified. They are often presented to a prospective buyer as a mixture of well-known breeds, such as "shepherd mix" or "poodle mix." Some traits, such as size and temperament, are difficult to predict in young puppies, as random bred puppies may change drastically as they mature. Traits such as adult size, coat type, and temperament become easier to predict in older puppies. Random breds can be described as "surprise packages"; only time will reveal exactly what you have. That has its own charms.

Breed Profiles

The AKC has grouped all recognized breeds into seven categories based roughly on function and ancestry. (Miscellaneous is a transitional, not an official, group. Dogs in this group are not entitled to full registration privileges.) Because they are related, or built to do similar work, the breeds in each category share many traits of form and function.

The Pembroke Welsh corgi is a herding dog developed in Wales to drive geese and herd cattle.

HERDING BREEDS

Some herding dogs are bred specifically to round up and manage herds of livestock; behaviors such as stalking or heel nipping are part of the package. A headstrong nature comes with boundless energy and stamina, requiring an intensive commitment from an owner. Other herding breeds are selectively bred to guard and defend these herds. Herding breeds can be highly territorial, aggressive, and intolerant of strangers. They make ideal watchdogs, but their protective behaviors may be unpredictable and uncontrollable without consistent training and good socialization. They are very loyal and naturally affectionate and can be very demonstrative about this with their owners.

Herding Trials

IF YOUR PUPPY DISPLAYS A LOT OF NATURAL HERDING instinct, you might consider channeling this talent into competitive herding events. A number of U.S. organizations sponsor herding classes, trials, and tests and offer titles and certificates of achievement. At these events, the "herd" may be composed of sheep, cattle, llamas, or ducks. Dogs are judged on their ability to take direction as well as on their natural aptitude. Most events are open to all herding breeds and some working breeds.

HOUNDS

Hounds are some of the world's most ancient breeds and have plenty of wonderful qualities that make them good pets. They are elegant, fastidious, and naturally healthy. Many of these breeds are also low maintenance. They have traditionally been bred as hunting dogs because they have a strong predatory instinct and sense of smell. The twenty-two hound breeds currently recognized by the AKC vary drastically in size and shape, but they are

Lure Coursing

THE SPORT OF LURE COURSING IS DESIGNED TO TEST THE skills of sighthounds—hunting hounds who instinctively chase and catch prey. In lure coursing, an artificial lure, suspended from a pulley, stands in for the prey. Dogs are timed as they pursue this "quarry" around the course. Several organizations offer events for both novices and competitive titleholders. Both the AKC (http://www.akc.org) and the American Sighthound Field Association (http://www.asfa.org) sponsor events and offer lure coursing titles.

Excellent trackers, bloodhounds such as this one are also affectionate and outgoing, and they do well with children and other dogs.

all mentally and physically designed to track and catch prey. They can be a challenge to train, however, as they are easily distracted and may simply "tune out" human communications. They may impulsively chase any bird, squirrel, or ball that catches their attention. They are not always reliable with small animals and other pets. Leash training, obedience training, and a securely fenced yard are mandatory for these breeds.

NONSPORTING BREEDS

Nonsporting breeds come from a wide range of backgrounds, making it difficult to generalize about them. Some have been traditionally bred as companions. Others, such as dalmatians and bulldogs, were bred for a working function that has now become obsolete. Although the nonsporting breeds vary drastically in size, type, and heritage, all were designed to interact with humans in some capacity and are therefore characteristically sociable.

Much loved by moviegoers, dalmatians generally make good companions and dependable watchdogs.

SPORTING BREEDS

Like hounds, sporting dogs are natural hunters. Setters, spaniels, pointers, and retrievers are some of the world's most popular breeds. Unlike hounds, sporting breeds are generally very sociable and highly responsive to human direction. They also have a tremendous amount of energy and stamina. Their exercise requirements are significant as is their need for social interaction. They are tireless and have a strong natural resistance to harsh environmental conditions. This means that an Irish setter will still probably insist on a two-hour run in the park in the pouring rain.

TERRIER BREEDS

Hardy, courageous, and self-sufficient, ancient terrier breeds were expected to hunt, eradicate vermin, guard the home, and serve as entertaining companions. Although they were developed as working dogs, terriers function primarily as companions today. Thanks to their compact sizes, smart appearances, and vivacious personalities, terriers are popular. They can be the perfect choice for owners who have small living spaces, and they make great

Earthdog Trials

EARTHDOG TRIALS ARE SPECIALIZED EVENTS FOR *dachshunds and terrier breeds that "go to ground" in pursuit of game. The trial involves testing the dog's hunting aptitude, in this case tracking prey, usually a rabbit or rat safely secured in a cage, through a series of prefabricated tunnels. Dogs become eligible for a series of titles—Junior Earthdog, Senior Earthdog, Master Earthdog—as they complete increasingly complex tests. To learn more about these events, visit http://www.akc.org/events/earthdog/index.cfm or http://www.dirt-dog.com (GTG Tunnels).*

playmates for active children. Attentive and fearless, they can be brilliant watchdogs. However, a bored or neglected terrier may resort to compulsive barking, digging, or destructive chewing. Without early comprehensive socialization to other dogs, some terriers have the potential to become dog aggressive. Due to their strong predatory instinct, terriers generally cannot be trusted with other small animals in your home.

Toy Breeds

Toys come from a wide range of backgrounds. Some are miniaturized versions of hounds or terriers who retain many of the basic traits associated with their larger counterparts. Others were developed solely to appeal to human companions, so they are naturally attuned to human interaction, are highly sociable, and are adaptable to a wide range of lifestyle demands. Easily portable, they make great travel companions. Smaller breeds are also noted for their longevity; however, their small sizes decrease their resistance to weather conditions and increase their risks for accidental injuries and escapes.

Toys are often the best choice for someone who is not prepared to cope with the care requirements of larger dogs. Daily upkeep is relatively undemanding and inexpensive. This does not mean that small dogs don't require regular exercise and grooming—they do, and many of them can be even more energetic than larger dogs.

Working Breeds

This is a broad category comprising police dogs, sled dogs, guard dogs, and draft dogs traditionally bred to pull carts. Many of these breeds are naturally versatile because they have been bred to perform

Siberian huskies, working dogs developed to pull sleds over snow-covered terrain, need to be kept busy and active if you don't want them to get into trouble.

multiple jobs, such as hunting, guarding, tracking, and serving as a companion. The common denominator is that they are all designed to assist humans in some capacity. But their natural working skills can veer in unwanted directions without adequate training and human interaction. Owners must be prepared to supply firm and consistent training for working breed puppies, lest they grow into unmanageable adults. Although they vary in appearance, working breeds are generally large and sturdy. They possess high levels of stamina and endurance and a natural affinity for human contact.

Small, Medium, or Large?

Before choosing XS or XXL, make sure you are aware of the potential drawbacks. Living with a big dog can be complicated in unexpected ways. Not only do they need more room for exercise, but they also are not easily portable and thus require a serious commitment to training from a very young age.

Consider the following potential hurdles to owning a large breed:

- At maturity, some large dogs are notably bigger and stronger than many people are. Transporting a large dog to the veterinarian or to a groomer can be a challenge depending on the size of your car and your physical capabilities.
- Do you have room to store 50-pound sacks of dog food?
- Many canine care services really do "charge by the pound."
- Grooming, boarding, and veterinary care can be considerably more expensive for large dogs.

Extra small puppies come with their own set of complications:

- They are more fragile, which can make them a poor choice for homes with active children or large dogs.
- Some veterinarians are not as familiar with a small puppy's risks for drug sensitivities or reactions to routine anesthesia or vaccinations as they are with risks faced by medium and large breeds.
- They may not need a large fenced yard, but a securely fenced yard is crucial. Tiny puppies can effortlessly slip through gates and underneath fences.
- Little dogs require more supervision when they are outdoors. They are especially susceptible to predation by wildlife, and because of their low body weights, they have less tolerance for weather extremes. This can complicate the house-training process.
- Public dog runs or parks can put them at risk for attacks from larger, aggressive dogs.

Sex Distinction

There are sex-related behavior differences, traceable to bio-chemical factors that determine a puppy's sex. The nature and extent of these differences vary by breed. Generally, males are considered to be more dominant and assertive, and females gentler and more tractable. For some breeds, the opposite is true, and for others, trait differences are minimal. The sex of a puppy can make a difference if you are selecting a companion for another dog. In general, an older dog is more likely to accept a puppy of the opposite sex. Both sexes can be reliably house-trained and bond with an owner.

Coats and Colors—the Icing on the Cake

It can be tempting to pick a puppy solely on his appealing coat or color. Personal preference is certainly an important considera-tion. But this is not the same as shopping for hats or wallpaper. Dog coats come in many varieties—from the short, curly coats of poodles to the long, silky coats of Irish setters. Some dogs have no coat—as is the case with the hairless Chinese crested. The short coat of the Chihuahua makes this pint-size dog better suited for indoor living, whereas the thick, dense coat of the Samoyed protects against harsh, wintry winds in cold climates. Of course, double-coated dogs can be kept comfortable in hot cli-mates with air-conditioning, and shorthaired or hairless breeds can be bundled in sweaters or kept indoors in chilly locales.

Grooming is another issue. Consider the type of terrain in which you live: choosing a longhaired Afghan hound may create a nightmare for you if you live in a rural region, where debris from fields or wooded areas will continually become trapped in your dog's coat; similarly, it will be near to impossible to keep a

The beautiful heavy coats of Samoyeds such as this one are perfect for winter in the Siberian tundra, where the breed originated. Summer in places such as the American South is more challenging for double-coated dogs.

dog's white coat looking pristine if you live in an area prone to rain and mud. Your forethought shouldn't stop with the main body coat. Some breeds have combination coat types that introduce grooming needs you may not have anticipated. For instance, the hairless Chinese crested does have long, silky hair on the head, tail, and feet; and the schnauzer comes with furnishings (longer hair around the legs and muzzle) that must be kept free from debris and are somewhat susceptible to staining, though the body coat can be kept shorn to a low-maintenance style.

A golden retriever pup enjoys a swim in the lake. The oils that make a retriever's coat water-repellent can transfer themselves to your carpet and any furniture he's allowed on.

Some coats, such as those of retrievers, are naturally water-repellent and are insulated to resist heat and cold. Much of this weather resistance is due to natural coat oils, which also cause a

Maintaining the appearance of a Lakeland terrier's wirehaired coat may require the attention of a professional groomer. The advantage of having wirehaired dogs is that they shed less than other dogs do.

distinct doggy odor that is transferred from the dog to his bed and to your carpet and furniture. Bathing will diminish the odor, but it also strips the protective coat oils, so it shouldn't be done too frequently.

Short coats, such as those of boxers and Chihuahuas, are generally less complicated to groom, but they offer less protection against hot or cold weather. Single coats—a one-layered coat without an undercoat, such as that of the Italian greyhound—can be fine and thin, offering less protection from the cold and the sun (sunburn can be a risk). Some flat coats, such as those of the German shepherd and the Labrador, have both an outer coat and an undercoat. These double coats offer more insulation from the weather, but they shed more than long coats do. Frequent brushing and vacuuming is essential.

Wiry coats, such as those of terrier breeds, provide protection from rough terrain and extreme weather. Matting and shedding are less of a problem, but the grooming required to maintain their appearance and texture can be complicated. Unless you are prepared to learn how to do this, it can mean regular professional grooming. Clipping will permanently soften the texture, which will greatly diminish the coat's natural protective qualities.

Long coats are glamorous, but they also require the most grooming. If neglected for even a short time, they will mat. Many longhaired dogs, such as the Samoyed, possess double coats. Dead hair will simply collect in the undercoat, creating mats and secondary skin irritations from the dirt and moisture that become trapped next to the skin. Professional groomers charge hefty fees for special services such as dematting. Worst case scenario, the mats may need to be shaved off, which can permanently alter the hair's natural texture.

A standard poodle shares the warmth of its thick curly coat with a hairless sphynx cat. Some authorities claim that poodles are less likely to trigger an allergic reaction than other dogs may, but there's no guarantee this will be the case.

Hypoallergenic Coats

HYPOALLERGENIC *AND* NONSHEDDING *CAN BE* misleading terms. Every dog—even hairless breeds—will shed to some extent. No breed can be guaranteed not to provoke an allergic reaction. Firsthand research is indispensable if you plan to acquire a puppy because of his purported hypoallergenic quality. Spending time with a dog is the only way to be sure about this. Don't base your decision on a quick trip to the breeder; he or she usually will have several dogs (possibly of different breeds) and even other pets on the premises, which may stimulate your allergic reaction and make it difficult for you to evaluate your potential reaction to allergens from just one dog. Instead, visit the home of a friend who owns only the breed you want; stay long enough (which varies from person to person) to possibly trigger an allergic reaction.

Curly coats, often considered nonallergenic and nonshedding, can actually require substantial grooming and are not guaranteed to prevent allergic reactions. They must be brushed every other day to remove dead hair and prevent mats and need to be trimmed every six weeks to three months in order to maintain a tidy appearance.

Whether your puppy has a wire-haired coat, like this fox terrier's, or a smooth coat, a long coat, or a short one—or not much coat at all—you need to keep her well groomed.

3

Buying
a Puppy

Boxers appeal to people wanting playful, highly energetic pets.

Even the most sensible choice for your lifestyle will never work if the puppy's personality does not appeal to you. Research and advice can only steer you in the right direction. After that, you need to get some experience interacting with individual dogs and puppies.

Interview Owners

Once you have an idea of the type of puppy you want, get out and meet some dogs and, more important, talk to their owners. These conversations can provide a lot of insight into the realities of daily life with a particular breed. Most dog owners are proud to show off their pets. This may be as simple as stopping to chat with someone walking his or her dog on your street or in the park. Pet shops are also good places to find owners and their dogs. In some towns, owners of certain breeds organize regular get-togethers at local dog parks. Following are some topics to discuss.

Health Issues

Are there any particular health issues associated with this breed? This factor may be overplayed or underplayed, depending on the source. But you may want to rethink your breed choice if you hear the same problems described by many owners. Owning a dog requires some outlay for veterinary expenses, but huge vet bills and chronic illness should never be a typical aspect.

Training Challenges

Are there any special behavioral problems associated with the breed? Is the breed you're considering notorious for chewing up furniture, barking when left alone, or hurling herself over the fence and disappearing? House-training is always a major question, and some breeds are definitely more challenging in this respect. Find out what other owners have to say. Do most owners favor one particular training method? Expert dog trainers and average pet owners can vary in these assessments.

Grooming Demands

Do most owners of certain breeds opt for professional grooming? What does this usually cost? Grooming demands may be more complicated than you think. You are better off knowing the truth about unpleasant topics such as shedding, matting, doggy odor, and drooling ahead of time. Flat-faced dogs may need to have their faces washed regularly to prevent food and debris from accumulating in wrinkles. Short-legged dogs require more

A groomer attends to a bichon frise puppy, whose thick, light-colored coat requires regular care.

frequent bathing simply because they are closer to the ground. Some puppies who appear low maintenance may in reality be nothing of the sort.

Social Quirks

How does the breed you're considering get along with children or other pets? Some breeds may be too large or aggressive to be kept in a home with small children; others may be too fragile to be added to a household with rough-housing teenagers or other large-breed dogs. Neither situation is necessarily obvious at first glance. Most puppies can be socialized to other animals as long as they are introduced when the puppy is still young and curious about new experiences. Some enjoy the company of other dogs, and others are naturally aloof or have the potential to be territorial or dog aggressive. They may not be the best choice for an inexperienced dog owner. If you have other pets in the house—cats or birds, for instance—be aware that some dog breeds have a strong predatory instinct, so do careful research.

Puppy Sources

Once you've decided on the breed you want, you need to find a reputable source. For random breds and crossbreds, you may want to check with your local shelters and rescue groups. For a pure-bred, the AKC, national breed clubs, and local dog clubs all provide referral services for breeders and rescue groups. Veterinarians, groomers, and trainers are usually acquainted with local breeders and animal shelters. Dog magazines and Internet research can help, but do not select a breeder based on a classified ad or a Web site; some are merely a means of marketing poorly bred, mill-raised puppies.

Dog breeders invariably gather in droves at local weekend dog shows. This is a great place to find breeders and to look at hundreds of dogs in one place. Most breeders will provide a business card if you request it. Although they may not have puppies available, they are usually willing to answer questions and will not hesitate to mention both the good and the bad points of the breed. Their foremost priority is finding the right homes for their dogs.

Ask about basic terms of sale such as health guarantees and return policies. Most breeders and adoption services provide some form of sales contract, but this should never include excessive demands. If you are not interested in co-owning a puppy with the breeder, purchasing an expensive show dog, breeding, or showing a puppy, don't feel obligated to agree to such things to get a puppy. (A breeder may present co-ownership as a purchasing option, offering to sell the puppy at a reduced price in return for specific commitments from the buyer. This arrangement should never be entered into casually. In the long run, it can work out to be far more expensive than purchasing the puppy outright.)

It is possible to acquire a healthy puppy from a retail source. But buyers have no opportunity to implement any of the research recommended in this book, such as meeting a puppy's breeder, seeing the parents, or acquiring background information regarding temperament, ancestry, or health history. The fact that a puppy is healthy at the time of sale is no guarantee that genetically based problems won't surface later.

If possible, arrange to visit in person. Reputable breeders and adoption services will also want to meet you if they are considering placing one of their puppies in your home. Keep in mind that for most of them, this is a hobby, not a profession. Be reasonable. Arrive on time. Do not bring a contingent of friends, relatives, and other pets unless this has been agreed upon in advance. Do not overstay your welcome.

Prepare a list of questions. It is easy to become distracted visiting the dogs and forget to ask important questions: What kind of grooming equipment, food, toys, crates, fences, and gates

A group of corgis plays with the breeder. Affection between a breeder and her dogs is a very good sign.

are recommended? What are the grooming requirements (including recommended tools)? Do any special training or behavior issues commonly arise in puppies or adolescents, and what training method does the breeder prefer? Are there any behavior differences between male and female puppies? Does this breed have any known problems with vaccine reactions or allergies to common medications? If the breed is normally screened for certain health problems, make sure the parents have been tested and ask to see the results. If you plan to have the puppy neutered, when does the breeder recommend doing this? Does the breed have any special dietary requirements? Don't hesitate to ask about the breeder's return policy. Reputable breeders are always willing to take their puppies back under any circumstances—but this does not always include a refund.

Check out all the breeder's dogs—not only the parents but any dogs the breeder has kept from previous litters as well. The adults should appear clean, healthy, and well fed, signs that the breeder takes proper care of the animals. They should also be relaxed and affectionate with the breeder (even breeds naturally shy or wary of strangers), signs indicating that the breeder properly socializes the puppies.

Your exhaustive research may lead you to a particular breeder or a puppy outside your local area. A long-distance purchase complicates matters a bit, but don't let it dissuade you from going with the right choice. Before finalizing the deal, be sure to have some phone contact with the seller; don't rely solely on e-mail. Request pictures of the puppy and, if possible, the parents and other related dogs. Ask for references from sources such as local veterinarians and dog clubs as well as from people who have previously adopted or purchased puppies from this source. The breeder should be prepared to furnish all the usual documentation that accompanies a puppy placement, including certification that a puppy is healthy at the time of sale, a sales contract, pedigree (family tree), and health records. The breeder should have ongoing records showing that the puppy's family has been tested for genetically based disorders commonly affecting the breed, such as hip X-rays or eye checks; the puppy's individual health records detailing health exams, vaccinations, deworming; or special testing if appropriate.

Picking Out a Puppy

Now that you have done your homework to determine the right type of puppy and to locate the right source, you are ready for the fun part. Although you have anxiously awaited the day when you can pick out your puppy and take her home, do not be impetuous in your selection. Chances are the breeder or adoption group will be more than willing to offer advice to help you pick the right puppy for your personality and lifestyle. Their recommendations are based on extensive experience and should be a major factor in your final decision.

Shipping Puppies

IF YOU ARE BUYING FROM A DISTANCE, YOU WILL NEED to make arrangements to bring the pup home. Buyers are sometimes apprehensive about having a puppy shipped by air, but this may be the best alternative if long-distance travel is required. A direct flight, even if it's a long one, is much faster and thus less stressful than a lengthy car trip.

It may be cheaper and safer to purchase a round-trip ticket and personally pick up the puppy than to have her shipped to you. Round-trip airfare for a person is often cheaper than a one-way fare to ship a dog. It also gives you the opportunity to monitor the puppy throughout the flight. Plus, she can travel in the cabin in a carrier small enough to be stowed under the seat. If the puppy is too large for this (or if she is flying alone, regardless of her size), she will need to travel in a pressurized baggage compartment in the cargo hold. This is also safer (and sometimes less expensive) if you are on the flight as well. A flat rate excess baggage fee for a dog is far less expensive than freight per pound air cargo fees. And you can regularly remind the flight crew about your onboard puppy, which ensures diligent service.

Breed Evaluation

If you are getting a purebred, read your breed's official standard. The information pertains to all specimens of a breed, not just show dogs. It will help you evaluate important features, such as size, color, and coat, listing desirable as well as undesirable features. For instance, a Samoyed's hair should be stick straight and harsh, not soft, curly, or wiry. Unscrupulous breeders may claim that a faulty puppy is a valuable rarity and ask a higher price. There is a reason why terms such as *teacup* and *hairless* do not appear in the official Chihuahua breed standard! To a buyer,

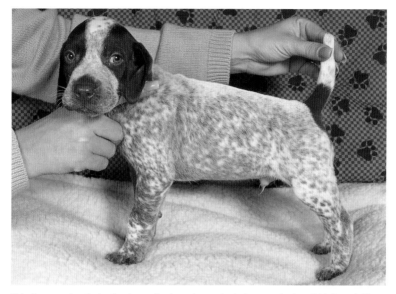

This German shorthaired pointer displays the typical characteristics of his breed. Know the breed standards before you begin looking for a puppy.

teacup means "extra small" and "extra cute"! However, teacup Chihuahuas are below the breed's standard size and are subject to significantly greater health problems.

Variation in some features such as size, coat color or type, and eye color may be nothing more than aesthetic imperfections (according to the breed standard). Consistency, not variation, is the hallmark of purebred quality. If most dogs have long tails, rest assured that the short-tailed puppy is not a "valuable rarity." Some faults are undesirable because they are linked to health problems. For instance, white coats and blue eyes have been linked to deafness in dogs. This is where your research can really pay off.

Temperament Evaluation

In their quest to accurately predict a puppy's future personality, behaviorists have devised formal criteria, known as temperament tests, to assess particular aspects of a puppy's evolving personality. Most of these tests were formulated to gauge the aptitude of a specific breed or type for a clearly defined job, such as candidates for guide dog or field trial training. Temperament tests vary but generally consist of a number of exercises such as:

- Social attraction—does the puppy spontaneously approach people, approach cautiously, act disinterested, or refuse to approach?

- Confidence—does the puppy approach without hesitation, stop to think first, or run away when faced with an unfamiliar object?

- Touch sensitivity—does the puppy remain calm, ignore the test, or begin to object as her toes are held and massaged, gradually increasing in intensity?

- Reactivity—does the puppy act alert, startled, or frightened when she hears an unfamiliar sound?

- Reaction to restraint—does the puppy struggle to get loose, calmly accept the situation, or display fear when she is picked up, held, and restrained?

Many breeders perform such temperament tests when the puppies are approximately seven weeks of age. These are not pass-or-fail tests but assessments meant to identify personality traits such as activity level, dominance, independence, sensitivity, sociability, and trainability. The results help a breeder match puppies with potential owners. If the puppies have been tested, the breeder will likely go over the results with you, possibly suggesting which puppy would fit well with your lifestyle. These tests are not infallible, however; results vary, for instance, due to breed-specific tendencies. Some breeds are naturally more independent or energetic, which will be reflected in their test scores. Keep in mind, too, that a puppy's temperament remains a work in progress until adulthood. If anything, temperament tests are useful in identifying puppies who may benefit from more socialization.

Even without a formal test, you can get an idea of a puppy's personality by observing her in her home territory. How does she react to strangers? Is she curious, disinterested, withdrawn, or fearful? How does she interact with her littermates? It's natural to be attracted to the most outgoing, active puppy, but give serious thought to what it will be like to live with this personality on a daily basis.

Keep in mind that it is normal for a puppy to prefer familiar people to strangers. Before deciding that a puppy is shy, give her a chance to approach you, and watch her reactions to treats, praise, and unfamiliar objects.

Look for a Healthy Pup

Evaluate the puppy's overall health. She should not be excessively fat or thin, although puppies generally have a more rounded shape than adults do. Puppies also normally have an abundance of loose skin, which they gradually grow into. The skin and coat should not look greasy, flaky, patchy, or dull.

Observe the puppy's actions. Puppies are by nature somewhat uncoordinated, but they should walk and run without any sign of pain, limping, or disorientation.

Take a look at how the puppy is put together. The proportions of various body parts will show if she is sturdy and properly constructed. Except in a few specialized breeds such as bulldogs or Pekingese, the back legs should be farther apart than the front legs. The front legs should line up under, not in front of, the pup's shoulders to support her body weight (a dog's center of gravity). Her rib cage should make up at least half the length of her body

This dalmatian puppy looks alert and healthy. Before buying a dog, carefully examine the pup for signs of illness or physical problems.

between shoulders and hips, and it should have a nicely rounded shape, not narrow or flat. Her elbows should be held close to the body, not obviously sticking out to the sides. She should not hesitate to put weight on her back legs. The tips of her back toes should line up approximately under her buttocks when her rear hocks are perpendicular. The rear hocks should not turn noticeably in or out. Her back should be level, not obviously high or low at either end. The tail should be a normal length and shape and free of kinks.

Examine the puppy's body. Check the abdomen for lumps that may indicate a hernia. A hernia is not always serious, but surgical correction may be required. By the time a male puppy is eight weeks of age, you should be able to confirm that he has two testicles. Puppies can retract their testicles until they reach adolescence, but you should be able to find them. Undescended testicles won't affect a puppy's health, but the condition will make neutering more complicated.

The puppy's head and face should be symmetrical. The muzzle, face, and ears should not have any crusty or bare patches. If they do, the pup may have demodectic mange, a condition caused by a microscopic parasitic mite in the hair follicles. It mostly affects puppies three to twelve months old.

The eyes should be clear and bright, with no watering or squinting. The whites should be white. The irises may be bluish gray and won't change to their normal color until puppies are four to six weeks old. Obvious injuries or infections will be easy to spot; inherited eye problems such as progressive retina atrophy (PRA) cannot be spotted without a professional exam at a later age.

This Saint Bernard's eyes are clear and bright. Always check for signs of eye problems.

By eight weeks, the puppy should have a complete set of puppy teeth. Crooked teeth are a fault but will not affect health or quality of life. Unless the puppy is teething, the gums should be free of swelling or redness. And the pup should have lovely "puppy breath," not breath that is excessively stale or pungent, which can indicate gastrointestinal problems.

Make sure the puppy can breathe comfortably through her nose when her mouth is closed, with no noisy, labored breathing; coughing; gagging; or nasal discharge. (Even flat-faced breeds should have quiet, unobstructed breathing.) Contrary to popular myth, neither a cold, wet nose nor a dry one is a reliable indication of health status. Gently press on the puppy's throat. If this triggers coughing, she may have kennel cough, a respiratory disease caused by bacteria (and sometimes by viruses or a combination of both) that may require medication.

Ears should be symmetrical, inside and out. The inside of the earflap and ear canal should be dry, pale pink, and odorless. Redness, scratching, head shaking, odor, or discharge indicates a problem.

If you have questions about the puppy's condition, ask before you take her home. Even if she seems fine, this cursory exam should be followed up with a full veterinary exam within a few days of bringing her home.

Papers

The acquisition of a puppy is generally accompanied by a sheaf of papers, whether from a breeder, a veterinarian, an adoption group, or a recognized kennel club. You should understand exactly what these are, regardless of whether you are purchasing a purebred or a random bred, a pet or a show dog. You will definitely need to refer

Carefully look at the teeth and gums of the puppy you're interested in buying. The teeth should be well formed and the gums a healthy pink, like those of this basset hound.

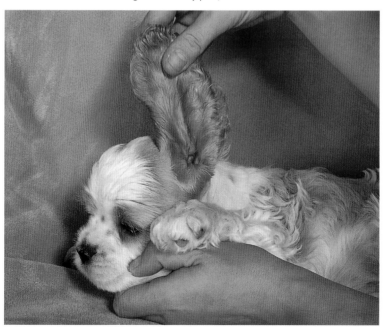

This cocker spaniel's ears show no signs of illness. Examine a puppy's ears for discharge or odor.

to at least one of these documents and the vaccination record, and you may need to refer to one or more of the other documents at a later date. Do not dismiss their importance.

The sales contract is to protect the puppy. It outlines the rights and responsibilities of both buyer and seller to ensure the protection of the only helpless party in the transaction: the puppy. The contract should outline care and treatment essential to the puppy's well-being. For instance, it may state that the puppy is not to be allowed to run loose, must not be kept in an outdoor kennel situation, and must have normal routine veterinary care and grooming. Most important, the contract should detail arrangements for returning the puppy if the buyer cannot keep her.

The true value of a contract, whether lengthy and complicated or basic and brief, ultimately depends on the integrity of the parties involved. If you have misgivings about a seller or about a puppy, a contract is not going to make any great difference. Do not buy the puppy. If you don't fully understand the contract, ask for clarification. Never assume that the terms can be altered or ignored after the sale. Litigation over dog-related problems is not infrequent and can be extremely costly.

Puppy Prices

Puppy prices will vary depending on geographic location and the breed of puppy you are seeking. The highest or lowest priced puppy is not necessarily going to be any better or worse than another. Most shelters and rescue groups charge fees to cover their operating expenses, and these can also vary widely. Find out exactly what is included in the adoption fee. This may range from nothing to a basic health guarantee to shipping, neutering, deworming, and vaccinating.

Beware of any breeder or adoption service representative who quotes outlandish prices or different prices for the same puppy. No reputable seller charges extra money for registration

Papers You Should Receive

WHEN PURCHASING A PUPPY, YOU SHOULD RECEIVE THE *following papers:*

- *Sales contract*
- *Health certificate*
- *List of vaccinations and deworming the puppy has received, dates when next treatment is due*
- *Instructions for feeding, grooming, general care*
- *Registration application or certificate*
- *Records of parents' health testing*
- *Pedigree*

You may not be particularly concerned with a puppy's registration and pedigree, but you should still inquire about them. Ascertain which registry is most commonly used for the breed. Not all registries are equal, and there is never any guarantee that certifications issued by one registry will be accepted by others. If a breeder habitually registers his or her dogs with obscure or alternate registries, this should arouse suspicion. The registration application or registration certificate must be issued by an official registration service to be valid.

If there is a reason a breeder does not intend to furnish registration papers with a purebred puppy, you should be informed of this prior to the sale. Breeders sometimes withhold papers until they receive proof that nonbreeding-quality puppies have been neutered. Or they may provide a "limited" registration for puppies who are not intended for breeding or show; in this case, the new owner can still register the puppy, and the breeder can later reverse this status if desired. Either way, you should be aware of this before purchasing the puppy.

Golden retrievers such as this one bring their new families years of great companionship, loyalty, and affection.

A young owner appears happy with her new boxer.

papers or offers a choice of papers for different prices. Nor should anyone demand prices associated with qualities they are in no position to guarantee.

The highest prices are generally found in retail pet shops, the lowest in classified ads or Web sites. The prices charged by reputable breeders fall somewhere in between. The difference is that a pet-quality puppy from a serious breeder is still the product of a carefully planned breeding program, and the expertise of the breeder is always available because he or she has a personal stake in each puppy.

4

Bringing Your Puppy Home

A puppy peers out of a carrying crate—an essential item for transporting your pup.

ADVANCE PLANNING NOT ONLY ENSURES THAT YOU will end up with the right puppy but also guarantees that you will be ready when you bring him home. You will need to shop for supplies, puppy proof the house, decide on a schedule for daily care, find a veterinarian and possibly a groomer, and find a puppy training class.

Selecting the Basic Equipment

One little puppy can require an amazing range of accessories, which are available in an overwhelming assortment of choices. Breeders and adoption services will provide recommendations for equipment based on personal experiences. They not only will know which brands are best for their puppies but also can tell you the best places to buy these items as well. Keep in mind, however, that this is not the time to splurge on expensive collars, leads, sweaters, or dog beds. Puppies can be counted on to ruin these items long before outgrowing them. "Durable, washable, and replaceable" is the mantra for puppy accessories.

Toys

There are millions to choose from, but not all toys are safe. Before you buy, make sure the toys are appropriate for your puppy's age and breed. Stuffed toys and latex squeakies that may be safe for small breed puppies are not recommended for large breeds. Don't overwhelm your pup with toys. Too many at one time can make it hard for a puppy to learn the difference

A Cardigan Welsh corgi lays claim to a soft, colorful, and safe puppy toy. Make sure the toys you choose are safe for your puppy.

between acceptable and unacceptable items for play. And make sure that the toy actually appeals to the puppy. Otherwise, the table legs will remain fair game.

Lightweight Collar and Lead

Start with a nylon collar that can be adjusted as the puppy grows and replaced as needed. (Since the collar will need to be replaced several times before your puppy reaches his adult size, wait until he is full-grown to splurge on fancy jeweled or leather collars.) Make sure there are no seams or rough edges that can irritate skin or become caught in hair. The collar should be large enough so that you can slip a couple of fingers comfortably under it, but the puppy should not be able to slip his head or foot through the opening. Purchase a small ID tag for the collar, so your pup can be easily identified if he accidentally strays from home. Even if the puppy is microchipped or tattooed (ask your veterinarian for information on these procedures), a tag is a good safety precaution. It may be possible to trace a puppy's owner through the information on a rabies tag or dog license, but an ID tag with your phone number greatly increases the chance that someone will contact you if your puppy becomes lost. Make sure it's the right size—a tag suitable for a Great Dane will weigh down a Yorkshire terrier.

It is better not to use pinch or choke collars (see box). Retractable leads also are not recommended for young puppies. They can easily become tangled in these extremely long leads, a potentially dangerous situation. A 6-foot lead is plenty long for leash training and walks. For small breeds, quarter-inch width is good; larger puppies will need one-half to 1-inch widths, depending on the size and strength of the dog. Make sure the clip that attaches

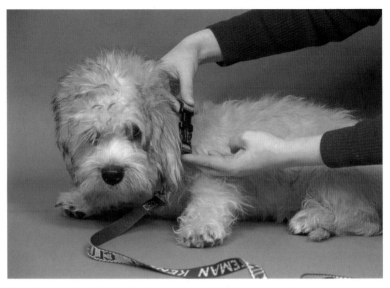

The collar worn by this Dandie Dinmont terrier is lightweight and loose enough not to choke the puppy.

the leash to the collar is large and strong enough to withstand any pulling by your dog but not so large that it is cumbersome.

Crate

Select a crate that is secure, sturdy, durable, and easy to clean. Puppies will be more reluctant to use a crate as a bathroom if it is small (see chapter 8 for crate-training): choose one large enough for the puppy to stand up and turn around in, but not large enough to take a stroll in. Do not purchase an adult-size crate for your puppy. (An exception is a large crate model that includes a removable divider, which cuts the floor area in half for the puppy stage.)

Some puppies can chew through thin plastic or wooden crates, so metal types may work better. The bars of these crates should be closely spaced so the puppy cannot get a foot or jaw stuck. Wire crates permit more air circulation and thus work par-

No Pinching or Choking

PINCH, OR PRONG, COLLARS AND CHOKE, OR CHAIN, *collars are sometimes used during training—something you'll be doing a lot of with a new puppy—but they are often used incorrectly and can easily cause permanent damage to your puppy's throat. A number of authorities believe they should not be used at all. However, if you do use one, never do so without the supervision of a professional trainer, and remove the collar immediately after the training session. It is very easy for a dog of any age to catch a link of the collar on something and choke himself.*

ticularly well for breeds prone to overheating. Some styles can be conveniently folded flat for storage. Aluminum crates are the top of the line and by far the most expensive; they're lightweight, sturdy, rustproof, and easy to clean.

Other breeds, those who are sensitive to cold or prefer more privacy, do better in fiberglass or plastic crates, which keep out drafts and are easy to disinfect. These usually come as two molded pieces that must be screwed together. Fold-up, collapsible plastic crates are not recommended. They can be dangerous because puppies can learn how to get these open from the inside or manage to collapse the crate onto themselves when attempting an escape.

Soft, mesh crates look nice, but any dog—especially a small puppy—can easily escape from one of these. This model is only safe for dogs who are already crate trained.

You may need to upgrade to a larger crate as your puppy grows. Keep in mind, though, that a crate *too* large will encourage crate soiling, a habit that's hard to break.

Bedding

This should be plain, durable, and washable. Avoid decorative wood and wicker beds and beds stuffed with foam or kapok. Even toy-size puppies can chew wicker and foam beds. Once chewing starts, it's nearly impossible to stop. Puppies won't hesitate to eat kapok or bits of wood. This behavior can lead to choking or intestinal blockage.

Dishes

Ceramic or stainless steel dishes are more durable than plastic types. Recent studies have shown that raised dog feeders, once recommended for large breed puppies, actually do not help prevent bloat. Weighted, nonspill dishes are a little more expensive but well worth the investment. You will be spending enough time cleaning without the added chore of cleaning up spilled food and water.

Food

Purchase the same brand of food that the puppy is already accustomed to eating. Arbitrarily switching a puppy's diet may trigger digestive upsets. Treats should be offered in moderation. Stick to one brand at a time so if the puppy has some kind of reaction, at least you will know what caused the problem.

Grooming Equipment

Brushes and combs should be appropriate for your puppy's coat type. Purchase shampoo specifically formulated for dogs; a dog's skin has a different pH level than a human's, so products sold for use on humans may be too harsh for your pet. Avoid flea or medicated shampoos unless recommended by your veterinarian as

Held gently but firmly, this bichon frise pup is groomed with a special comb.

these products can be toxic and irritate skin. Look for a small, scissors-type nail trimmer designed especially for puppies. And don't forget dental care: small, toy, or puppy-size toothbrushes make the job much easier (again, use toothpaste made for dogs).

Cleaning Products

This is where you can splurge—and don't underestimate what you will need. This will include many, many rolls of paper towels, spray disinfectants, stain removers, deodorizers, and spot cleaners for rugs and upholstery. If the puppy is not yet house-trained, you will also need a supply of house-training pads, a litter box, or a stash of newspapers. (See chapter 8 for tips on house-training.)

Gates and Pens

Confinement is necessary for your puppy's safety. Before you bring him home, arrange a containment system both indoors and outdoors. A crate is fine for short periods of time, but for most of the day your puppy will need freedom to exercise, socialize, and interact with you. At the same time, you will need a reliable way to restrict his access to certain parts of the house. Otherwise, it will be impossible to keep an eye on him and make sure he is not getting into trouble. For your puppy's safety (and for your peace of mind), do not rely on makeshift barriers. Pet supply companies offer many styles of puppy pens and temporary gates that are useful as indoor barricades. Outside, fenced yards should be thoroughly inspected to make sure there are no gaps that small puppies can squeeze through. Some puppies are climbers or jumpers; others will try to dig or burrow underneath or may chew wood or plastic gates.

Two exuberant cocker spaniels and their human playmate have lots of room to jump around in this indoor pen.

Puppy Proofing Your Home

Puppy proofing an entire house is unrealistic. It is far easier and safer to puppy proof a couple of rooms and implement some means of keeping the pup out of the rest of the house. You cannot supervise a puppy who has access to the entire home. Unsupervised access will make house-training impossible—and it is dangerous. In general, places such as garages, basements, workrooms, and tool sheds pose the greatest hazards for puppies, and a secure door is your best option.

If the puppy is going to spend time outdoors, ornamental gardens and valuable shrubbery should be fenced off. Puppies have no appreciation for beautiful landscaping and will cut a path of destruction through your yard. Garden decor can also present many hazards. A puppy can be injured climbing on or jumping off walls, planters, birdbaths, fountains, pools, and decks. Pesticides, herbicides, fertilizers, deck sealant, and even some plants can be toxic. Consuming garden mulch or decorative gravel can cause choking or intestinal blockage.

Although it may seem less risky and less messy to confine the puppy to a playpen or kennel run, he must have social contact and opportunities to observe the household routine. Inside, kitchens or family rooms are usually good choices. However, be aware that most puppies will not hesitate to eat anything that smells or tastes interesting, and they can ingest fatal amounts of household cleaning products, pesticides, and insecticides that have been applied to surfaces inside or outside of the home. Be sure to remove these products from the area your pup is confined to, or at least secure them in a locking cabinet. Outside, a secure fence is a must. Puppies have limited attention spans and almost no concept of distance; stairways, pools, decks, hot tubs, and balconies should be off-limits. Confining your puppy to a safe part of the yard helps protect him from hazards such as ingestion of poisonous plants, choking on small toys or other objects he may find if allowed to roam freely, and accidental electrocution.

A Question of Balance

ALL PUPPIES ARE ENERGETIC AND INQUISITIVE, BUT their modus operandi can take many forms. Some are diggers, some are climbers, and some are more prone to chew or swallow foreign objects. A puppy's ability to understand danger and use caution is not inborn; it is learned. Nothing will be safe during this learning process, but without these experiences, he cannot develop a reliable frame of reference about his environment. So, protect your puppy from danger and supervise his activities, but let him explore his world.

Finding a Veterinarian

One of the most important tasks to accomplish before bringing your puppy home is finding a veterinarian. Don't neglect to do this, even if the puppy appears healthy. Many sales and adoption contracts stipulate that a veterinarian must examine the puppy within a specified time. This is a sensible precaution for the puppy, the new owner, and the seller.

If you obtained your puppy locally, the breeder, adoption service, shelter, or store can usually recommend a local practitioner. Ask for recommendations from other dog owners, too. Or, do your own investigating and comparison shopping. Call several clinics and compare fees for typical services. Ask questions: How

A corgi explores the many wonders of his new backyard. A puppy's activities should be closely supervised to ensure his safety.

long is the average wait for an appointment? Pets rarely provide advance notification of illness, and emergency services should not be your only choice in these situations. Does the clinic provide twenty-four-hour emergency services? Are hospitalized pets monitored overnight? Will you be able to see the same doctor for each visit? This is not always the policy for large, busy clinics, but it has definite advantages. A regular doctor will be acquainted with the details of your dog's medical history, his growth and development, and his personality. And the puppy will feel more comfortable and less likely to develop a fear of going to the veterinarian if he always sees someone familiar.

Visit potential clinics. Does the office appear clean and well managed? Do the staff members relate well to the animals? Are they helpful and personable to the clients? Are the premises secured to prevent possible escapes from cages or dog runs?

You should also meet the prospective veterinarian. Do you feel comfortable talking to this person? You may need to ask about treatment options, fees, drug interactions, and referrals. The veterinarian is there to answer your questions. You should feel confident that this doctor is sincerely interested in your pet's welfare. You should not feel pressured, confused, or intimidated. Nor should the doctor be too busy to talk to you or to return your phone calls. Top-quality care is not possible without good communication.

A veterinarian examines an American Eskimo dog. Before taking your puppy for his first checkup, inspect the clinic and talk to the veterinarian to make sure that your pet will receive good care.

The Puppy's First Veterinary Visit

A ROUTINE CHECKUP SHOULD BE SCHEDULED WITHIN A few days of your puppy's arrival. This assures everyone that the puppy is in good health and allows you to plan a schedule for routine vaccinations and preventive care. Be sure to bring along vaccination records and information on any other treatments received. This not only ensures that the puppy receives treatments on schedule but also prevents risks associated with repeating them unnecessarily. Puppy vaccinations will not trigger any immune response if they are administered less than three weeks apart. Too many vaccinations in too short a time may suppress a puppy's immune system and raise the potential risks associated with vaccine reactions. Similarly, extra doses of puppy deworming medications can be toxic. If you are considering having your puppy microchipped for identification, your veterinarian should use a microchip scanner to ensure that the procedure has not already been done.

The Homecoming

If you are buying from a breeder, you may be allowed to visit your puppy before he is eight weeks old, but don't expect to bring him home before this age. Eight-week-old puppies are better prepared physically and mentally to cope with stress. They are larger and stronger with a more mature immune system. They are also fully weaned and have had at least one puppy vaccination.

Adjusting to a new home is a tremendous transition. If possible, arrange to devote several days to getting your new puppy settled in and accustomed to your house rules. Don't forget to account for "alone time" in the puppy's daily schedule. He will undoubtedly be the center of attention when he first arrives, which can give him the idea that constant attention is normal.

Undaunted by the puppy's size, a young girl has picked up her Samoyed to lavish affection on him. Sammies, like most dogs, crave lots of attention from their owners.

From day one, introduce the puppy to his crate or his partitioned area where he can spend some time alone for a few minutes. Gradually increase the amount of alone time. Eventually, everyone will be going back to work or school, and the puppy must be able to adjust to spending time on his own.

The First Day

Some puppies will walk into a new home and act as if they have lived there forever. Others may take a while to adjust. In the latter case, situate the puppy in a safe, quiet part of the house. Don't overwhelm him with attention before he's ready. Give him time to gain confidence and get his bearings. Speak softly and reassuringly, and let him decide to come to you. Don't expose him to the stress of meeting new people or visiting new places. If the puppy does not yet come reliably when called, take him outside only on a lead. Chasing him around the yard to catch him will only add to his confusion and anxiety.

Some puppies will react with boundless excitement and curiosity. They will want to meet everyone and investigate their new surroundings from the moment they arrive. Such enthusiasm is infectious, but this is the time you must set boundaries and stick to your prearranged routine. Just like children, puppies can become so overwhelmed that they forget to eat or sleep. They can become cranky, disoriented, and stressed.

Daily Routines

For the first week, concentrate on getting the puppy into a routine for eating, sleeping, and eliminating. Dogs are creatures of habit and relish consistency. Stick to the puppy's established feeding times as closely as possible, and always feed him in the same place, with water available at all times. You may need to take your puppy outside several times a day to eliminate until he is house-trained. Designate an appropriate place in your yard and return to the same spot each time. (See chapter 8 for house-training tips.) Decide on a sleeping place where the puppy can be safely confined throughout the night.

A Great Dane pup is introduced to his water bowl and papers, which are neatly tucked away in a corner.

Introducing the Puppy to the Household

Your puppy's arrival will include meeting the rest of the family, and you may need to use varied strategies when introducing him to his different family members.

Puppies and Caged Pets

Other animals usually fascinate puppies, but this interest may not be mutual. Supervise all pet interactions. In some cases, complete separation may be the simplest, safest option. A puppy may be too exuberant and accidentally injure small, fragile pets while trying to play with them. Puppies have fallen into fish tanks, and frightened parrots, hamsters, and tortoises have bitten them.

Puppies and Cats

Some puppies are already socialized to cats when they arrive in a new home, and some cats are unfazed by a puppy's presence. If not, supervised introductions are required. For the first meeting, keep the puppy either leashed or restrained. Make sure the cat has an escape route if she feels threatened. Watch the cat's expressions and body language for signs of fear or aggression. As long as the puppy seems curious but polite and the cat is calm, continue the introduction. Separate them if the puppy becomes too excited or if the cat becomes frightened. It might be best to keep them in separate rooms and repeat the introductions periodically until the cat gets used to the puppy's presence in the house. Some cats will choose to retreat rather than socialize with a puppy. In that case, you will have to accept the situation as it stands. Some puppies are simply too rough and boisterous to play with a cat, although maturity and training may improve the relationship.

Puppies and Other Family Dogs

Some adult dogs are naturally more sociable and will enthusiastically welcome a new puppy into the pack. Others, if not exactly delighted, at least have a tolerance for puppies—but not all of them do and will warn a puppy off. A puppy cannot be counted on to understand another dog's warning and may get things off on the wrong foot by trying to play. Canines communicate by using exaggerated gestures to emphasize their moods. Puppies begin learning these signals from their dams when they are just a few weeks old, but they need months of practice to master them. They cannot be depended on to interpret and appropriately respond to another dog's messages. As pack leader, this is your role in the introduction process.

Before you introduce the dogs to each other, consider their relative sizes and ages. A very small or elderly dog should not be expected to tolerate the antics of a rambunctious puppy. Some dogs may be aggressive. Don't try to force a friendship. Gradual introductions and supervised visits may lead to an amicable relationship. And never introduce a new puppy by plopping him right into another dog's home turf. This can set the stage for territorial aggression before either dog makes a move.

A puppy often acts submissively when first meeting an adult dog. He uses body language to make himself look small and nonthreatening, such as crouching or crawling, head down, ears flattened back, and tail carried low and wagging stiffly. He may avert his gaze from the larger dog or twist his neck to the side, whine or nuzzle the other dog's mouth, or roll on his back. If the puppy seems overly anxious or intimidated (indicated by panting, shaking, or trying to hide), end the visit.

The adult dog might display dominant behaviors, intended to make himself look bigger through a combination of high head

A group of adult dogs calmly greet a newcomer, a young Shetland sheepdog.

carriage, arched neck, erect ears, and tail carried high, with a rapid, stiff wag to advertise confidence. A dominant dog may stand over his rival with his front feet on the other dog's back, or he may close his jaws around the subordinate's muzzle.

You must put each dog's gestures and body language into context to accurately gauge what each is thinking. A crouching dog may appear submissive, but this takes on an entirely different meaning if this posture is accompanied by defensive growling. Look, listen, and size up the dynamics of the situation before concluding that the dogs are getting along.

At first, keep both dogs leashed and just let them look at each other. If they seem calm, happy, and interested, let them approach each other, but you should keep physical control. Talk to them reassuringly, and stop if either one becomes fearful or agitated. Encouraging them with toys or food rewards may not be a good idea because it can trigger rivalry.

If both dogs continue to act neutral or friendly, let them touch and sniff. This usually leads to tail wagging. One or both might begin displaying obvious dominant or submissive gestures. This should not be a problem as long as the dominant dog responds appropriately to the other dog's submissive behavior. Monitor their gestures closely because these can change instantly. If you see any tension or hostility, end the visit.

A series of gradual introductions may be needed before the dogs feel comfortable together. Until you are certain that they are going to get along, you must have a way to keep them separated when they cannot be supervised. You should have a safe method for intervening so you won't be injured. Owners who have tried to separate fighting dogs by jumping into the fray have been bitten by their own pets.

Pitfalls to Avoid

GIVEN TIME, DOGS USUALLY WORK OUT AN ACCEPTABLE social arrangement among themselves. Human efforts to speed up the process can make matters worse by instigating rivalries and dominance problems.

- *Do not force a fearful dog to approach or make eye contact with a dominant dog.*
- *Do not try to apply your own ideas of generosity, fairness, and sharing.*
- *Do not encourage an older dog to share his toys, bed, or food with the puppy.*
- *Do not allow the older dog to feel slighted or neglected in favor of the new puppy.*

Puppies and Children

Children should feel that they are personally responsible for part of the puppy's daily care. This encourages bonding and helps the child understand that the puppy is more than an entertaining plaything. A child's age must be taken into consideration when allotting these chores. Puppy care requires patience, sound judgment, and a degree of physical strength. If a child is too young to take responsibility for feeding, walking, or grooming, he or she can still be in charge of daily cuddling and petting.

If a puppy is not accustomed to children, their introduction may take a few days. Young children are generally active and noisy, and puppies may interpret their normal exuberance as threatening. The introduction process should be calm, quiet, and supervised. It is probably safest to have the child and puppy sit on the floor. Let the puppy come to the child voluntarily. Show the youngster how to extend a hand for the puppy to sniff or offer a treat or toy. Encouraging the child to feed the puppy some treats usually gets the ball rolling. Teach the child to speak softly to him, reach slowly, and avoid startling him. Never let a child grab the puppy, chase him, corner him, or attempt to pick him up. If the puppy becomes nervous or agitated, conclude the visit.

One of the most important lessons to teach a child is how to pick up the puppy safely, supporting his weight and holding him close to the body. If the puppy is resistant to being picked up

A girl brushes her Shetland sheepdog. If children are old enough, they should be given puppy care tasks such as feeding and grooming.

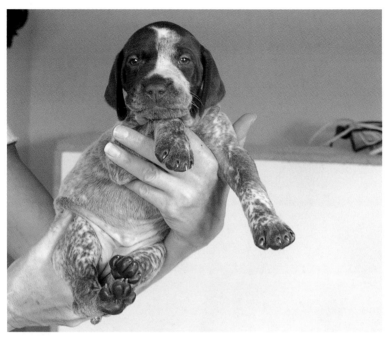

When picking up a puppy such as this German shorthaired pointer, you need to give her proper support. Before letting a child pick up a puppy, make sure the child knows the correct method.

or is too heavy for a child, don't encourage the idea at all. A fearful puppy can bite, and one bad experience will set the stage for future problems.

A child may not realize some forms of play are too rough or possibly threatening to a puppy. Overexcited puppies can nip, scratch, or knock a child down. This can happen accidentally during play or as a matter of self-defense. Biting, snapping, and jumping are far more difficult to discourage if a puppy resorts to these actions because he feels threatened. Every dog has the capability and potential to bite under the right (or wrong) circumstances. Dogs rarely bite without provocation or warning, but a child may not be able to understand warning signals. Incidents can occur at any time, which is why supervision is needed.

Your puppy should always have access to a bed or a crate when he needs a break from playing. Children should be taught to respect a puppy's need to retreat. When the puppy retires to his resting place, he is off limits.

Introducing Your Puppy to the Neighborhood

Puppies who have not received all their vaccinations can contract an illness just about anywhere, but areas frequented by large numbers of dogs present the greatest risk—dog parks, grooming salons, dog shows, and boarding kennels. Avoid these places until the puppy is fully vaccinated. This does not mean that it's OK to keep your puppy isolated during this time. Between eight and sixteen weeks of age, he needs regular introductions to new people, places, and things. Introduce the puppy to visitors at home or in locations that don't attract too much dog traffic.

Some puppies may need a gradual introduction to unusual aspects of their new environment. A first encounter with things such as horses, elevators, and traffic noises can be very startling. Do it slowly, but don't postpone it.

A young owner takes her rottweiler on an introductory walk through the new neighborhood.

5
Life with
Your Puppy

A sheltie enjoys a very large rope toy.

Your puppy depends on you for many things. Regardless of how your day is going, she will need to be fed, groomed, and walked. These simple, everyday chores have implications far beyond daily care. A regular routine is the foundation of bonding with your puppy, training her, and teaching her to understand her role in your family pack. Additionally, the time you spend with your puppy reminds you of why you wanted a dog in the first place: the stresses of your busy life melt away as the two of you unwind with a leisurely stroll through the park.

What's for Dinner?

It can be a challenge to make sure your puppy's diet is tasty, nutritious, and healthy. "Nutritionally balanced and complete" doesn't necessarily mean that every kind food is equally good for your puppy.

Dog food comes in two basic forms: canned and dry. Many owners feed these in combination to increase palatability and reduce risks associated with bloat. Although it is tasty, canned food has high water content, up to 75 percent. A tiny puppy may become full before she eats enough per meal to satisfy her body's nutritional needs. Although canned food is more expensive than dry food, it does have a longer shelf life. Many brands are packaged in single serving containers, perfect for small dogs.

Dry food is more economical than canned food and contains more protein, fat, and calories per serving, which can be good or bad depending on your puppy's individual requirements. It is convenient to feed, easy to store, satisfies a puppy's need to chew, and may contribute to dental hygiene.

Making the Right Choice

The simplest way to select a food is to use what the seller recommended when you got your puppy. If you decide to change your puppy's diet, this should be based on recommendations of experienced breeders or your veterinarian. Otherwise, there is no guarantee that a new diet will meet your puppy's nutritional requirements according to size and age. Casually experimenting or frequently switching brands may lead to a nutritional imbalance, house-training problems, and bad eating habits. If you need to switch, do it gradually over the course of a week, adding increasing amounts of the new food to each meal.

Your puppy may be allergic to certain foods, which becomes evident when you change her diet. Food allergies usually take the form of digestive disturbances, skin irritations, or

This Pekingese pup looks unhappy with her empty water bowl. Always make sure your dog has plenty of water.

occasionally, respiratory distress. It may take up to six weeks for problems to become obvious. If your puppy stops eating, conspicuously gains or loses weight, or develops bloat, gas, diarrhea, or a skin irritation, this may be a reaction to the new food. Many breeders recommend rice for puppies because it is more easily digested and is less likely to cause allergies than corn, wheat, and oats. Similarly, many breeders prefer dog foods made with exotic meats such as bison, elk, fish, or duck because these products are less likely to trigger food allergies.

Evaluating Foods

The simplest and safest approach is to select a complete, balanced commercial dog food. Your breeder or veterinarian may recommend a specific brand; otherwise, there are a wide variety of brands available in pet supply stores. Manufacturers have spent many years researching canine nutritional requirements,

A Question of Balance

WATER SHOULD ALWAYS BE AVAILABLE AND ALWAYS
kept in the same place. If the puppy is not acclimated to drink-
ing your local tap water, bottled water may be best for the first
few days. Gradually add more tap water to this until you are sure
the puppy will tolerate it. Make sure that the she drinks water
every day. Kennel-raised puppies don't always know how to
drink from a water dish and can become dehydrated before they
learn. Puppies normally learn how to lap water by emulating
their mother during weaning. In commercial kennel situations,
the dogs have only hanging water bottles, no dishes.

and they tailor the formulas of their foods to meet these needs. The ingredients of commercial foods are required to meet minimum nutritional levels set by the Association of American Feed Control Officials (AAFCO). Check the labels for the following information:

- Source of nutrients: Foods with identical percentages of various nutrients can differ drastically in taste and digestibility, depending on the ingredients. Not only do dogs generally prefer meat-based formulas to grain-based types when it comes to taste, but meat sources also provide better-quality protein. Foods that are predominantly grain based are less expensive than meat-based types, but they can cause deficiencies of protein and amino acids, zinc, or vitamin A in growing puppies.

- Order of ingredients: The AAFCO requires manufacturers to list all ingredients in descending order to designate the relative percentage of each one. The first three or four ingredients should be meat or meat based. Five or six types of grain should not follow one meat-type ingredient. Grain-based components should not make up most of the formula, regardless of the order in which they are listed on the label.

- Quality of ingredients: All meats are not equal. There is a big difference between meat, meat by-products, and meat meal. Make sure that the sources are clearly defined on the label. Some brands contain organic, natural, or human grade ingredients. These may or may not offer superior nutritional value even though they are usually more expensive. Ask your breeder or veterinarian if you are not sure.

- Expiration date: The date should be clearly printed on the bag. Do not purchase more dry dog food than your puppy will consume in three to four weeks. Kibble contains preservatives, but it will become rancid after the expiration date.

Puppy-Specific Formulas

Many breeders of large and giant breeds do not recommend foods "formulated for growing puppies." Although many of these dogs don't reach maturity until they are two years old, they do not grow at a uniform rate. Misjudging that rate and keeping a dog on puppy formula—which is higher in calories and fat—could exacerbate potential orthopedic problems by encouraging overly fast growth rates and obesity, which places undue stress on growing bones and joints. Giant breed puppies may fare better on the lower fat and protein formulas of adult diets; consult with your veterinarian, as this is a hotly debated topic.

Small breed puppy formulas are higher in fat and protein than are regular diets. Since many small breeds experience their major growth by four to five months of age and reach full size by six to eight months of age, such high concentrations could lead to obesity if the puppy is not gradually weaned to an adult formula as her growth rate slows.

Yorkshire terriers such as these and other small dogs may reach their full size sooner than large dogs do. Ask your veterinarian when you should adjust the diet from puppy formulas to adult formulas.

Vitamin/Mineral Supplements

Slight dietary imbalances can quickly affect a growing puppy. Feeding a nutritionally complete food is far easier than attempting to supplement an unbalanced diet. Supplementation can lead to vitamin toxicity or secondary deficiencies from imbalances. Supplementation should not be necessary if your puppy is fed a high-quality diet. If you prefer not to take chances, you can safely supplement your puppy's diet with healthy snacks, such as home-made dog treats and frozen vegetables. But vitamin and mineral supplements should be given only on a veterinarian's or breeder's recommendation.

Junk Food

Occasional treats are fine, but use common sense. Like human junk foods, snacks are tasty because they have a high fat and sugar content, but they are the number one culprits in causing canine obesity. Snack foods should never compose more than 10 percent of your puppy's daily diet.

Puppies will eat just about anything you offer them, including potentially dangerous foods intended for human consumption, such as onions, garlic, and chocolate. Although dogs love raw foods such as bits of meat or a bone with meat on it, the salmonella risk associated with them poses a far more serious danger for puppies. Raw or cooked, small or splintery bones are a choking hazard and should never be offered to dogs of any age. Do not offer puppies excessively large pieces of food; they might impulsively swallow such foods whole and choke. Avoid spicy or greasy foods, regardless of whether your puppy seems to like them. They can cause drastic dietary disturbances. Many puppies love coffee and alcoholic drinks, especially beer and wine. Both can be toxic to dogs, as are grapes and raisins.

Offered in moderation, treats and snacks will not cause indigestion or finicky eating habits. They should not, however, be offered in response to a puppy's whining and demanding. Use them to reward good behavior or to reinforce training. Set boundaries and let the puppy earn her reward.

When to Feed

The canine digestive system is designed to handle infrequent, large meals. Your puppy's ancestors were forced to hunt for each meal, fight for a share, and starve until the next kill. From birth, a puppy's survival hinges on the amount of food she can consume

A smooth fox terrier nurses two of her puppies.

in a competitive situation. Puppies eat until they are exhausted, not until they are full.

During weaning, they are fed as often as they want to eat. By the time a puppy is eight weeks old, her biological requirements have changed, and her eating habits should reflect this. Measured portions and regular feeding times help to establish good eating habits and house-training routines.

A puppy's most rapid growth occurs during weeks eight through twelve. During this period, she needs to consume two to three times the calories and nutrients of an adult dog and may need up to four meals a day (read the food bag's label for portion size). She will be unable to eat a day's worth of nutrients in just one meal. You may need to increase the recommended portion size during these weeks, but uneaten food should be picked up after twenty minutes.

Her growth will start to decrease after twelve weeks of age. Reduce the number of feedings by one, but slightly increase the portion size of the remaining meals. After six months of age, most medium to medium-large breeds are fine with one meal per day. For very large or very small breeds, however, splitting the day's food portion into two smaller meals is best. This method curbs large breeds' tendency to overeat, which can contribute to bloat and obesity. Small breeds have small stomachs and high metabolisms, so spreading out the meals helps maintain proper blood sugar levels and body weight. (This method does not apply universally; monitor your dog's weight regardless of breed, and keep her in the proper range for her size and breed.)

Reducing Risks of Bloat

GAS AND FLUIDS TRAPPED IN THE STOMACH CAN CAUSE a life-threatening condition called bloat (gastric torsion). The risk of bloat can be minimized by dividing food into two smaller daily portions, moistening kibble or mixing it with canned food, avoiding foods with citric acid preservatives, discouraging your puppy from eating too fast, and ensuring that your puppy remains calm and relaxed during and after mealtime.

How to Feed

A regular feeding routine allows for portion control and instills "table manners." Always feed your puppy in the same place—a quiet corner of the kitchen or in her crate works well as a "dining room." Intrusions and distractions during mealtime encourage bad eating habits. If a puppy feels nervous or threatened while eating, she may become protective of her food, eat too fast, or refuse to eat at all. If distracted, she may lose interest in eating and simply wander off.

The pace at which food is eaten varies from puppy to puppy. Some dogs bolt it down; others take their time. Both can be normal. As long as she consumes her food steadily, allow your puppy to eat at her own pace. However, even the slowest puppy should finish her food within ten to fifteen minutes. If the puppy picks at her food, don't encourage this behavior by making food constantly available; remove the dish after twenty minutes.

Feeding Problems

Many humans obsess about food, and this interest naturally extends to our pets. A puppy learns very early that food has many social and psychological connotations. Dysfunctional eating habits can take root early.

Overeating and Regurgitation

In a wild pack, dogs normally bolt down large quantities of food within a few minutes. They rarely chew, even when they have time to do so. Carnivore teeth are good for biting and tearing but ineffective for grinding food to bits. A dog's digestive system is built to overeat and quickly digest big meals.

It's not unusual for a puppy to consume a large meal and retire to her crate (or, as is sometimes the unfortunate case, *your* bed), regurgitate, and eat it at leisure. You may find this behavior objectionable, but it is not abnormal. Dogs have an extremely well-developed ability to regurgitate, thanks to their scavenging heritage. This operates as a protective mechanism. They tend to "eat first, think later," allowing them to regurgitate toxic substances or excessive amounts they have con-

Two American Eskimo dogs snarf down a dish of food. Puppies usually bolt their food and overeat; it's not unusual for them to then regurgitate it.

sumed. Puppies will regurgitate when they overeat or when they become overexcited or drink excessively after consuming a large meal. Less common instances are when they are stressed or when they are frightened—be aware that they are not above using this behavior as an attention-getting device.

If your puppy regurgitates on a regular basis, consult your veterinarian. If there is no underlying health problem, you will need to monitor her eating habits more closely. She may be consuming items that she should not when she is outdoors, or she may be allergic to something in her diet. You may need to cut her daily meal into two smaller portions. Or, she may simply need a less stressful mealtime environment. A puppy will need to go out to relieve herself after eating, but restrict strenuous exercise for an hour or two.

Choking on Food

A puppy can gag or choke if her kibble is too large or too dry or if she swallows too much at once. Choking can happen if a large puppy gulps a mouthful of small kibble. A tiny puppy can choke on a single piece of large-size kibble. Most of the time, a puppy manages to swallow or spit out any food she is choking on. If your puppy is actually choking, you may need to dislodge the obstruction (see chapter 6, first aid).

Moisten the kibble before feeding if your puppy regularly gags or chokes when eating, if she is prone to bloat, or if she is reluctant to chew due to the pain of teething. Soak the kibble in water for two to three hours before offering it to your pup. Another trick is to make a "kibble soup" by mixing the dry dog food with a combination of water or broth and bits of meat and vegetables.

Picky Eaters

Finicky eating habits are quickly learned because the reinforcements are so good. The anxious owner usually offers increasingly delicious fare, often at the puppy's request, and tops it off with lavish praise and attention if the puppy shows the slightest interest in eating.

From birth, puppies are conditioned to eat in a competitive situation, which also provides a psychological incentive to eat. Removing this natural motivation, such as when a puppy first leaves her littermates, can cause a temporary loss of interest in eating. This will resolve on its own if you don't encourage it. A finicky appetite can also result if a naturally timid puppy is stressed. She may become afraid to eat in the presence of anyone. This behavior can be avoided by getting the puppy accustomed to eating in her crate.

A sextet of dalmatians vie with each other for a platter of food. There's nothing finicky about these eaters.

Usually, puppies are not fussy eaters. A temporary loss of appetite can occur during teething or following vaccinations, but continual weight loss and poor appetite can indicate health problems and may signal the onset of a more serious disorder. Very often, lack of appetite is the earliest sign of illness. Unless you have trained your puppy to have good eating habits, you can easily miss this vital clue.

Food Guarding

One of the earliest lessons that a puppy learns is that access to food hinges on competition and pack order. It is natural for a puppy to guard her food from other dogs, but she should not guard her food from you—her pack leader. Your puppy should always allow any family member to approach or pick up her dish before, during, or after mealtime. Sitting near the puppy, talking to her, and petting her while she eats can prevent food guarding. Ignore protests, hand-feed her a few pieces of food, and reprimand any growling. She will soon learn that you have no intention of taking her food and, more important, that growling and snapping are not tolerated. If food guarding is a problem, it may be necessary to hand-feed the puppy all her meals until she accepts the idea that you control the food.

By holding her rottweiler's food dish while the dog eats, a young owner ensures that food guarding will not become a problem.

Begging at the Table

Puppies usually resort to whining and begging to get a taste of your food. This habit is already well established when you bring your puppy home, learned from her mother during weaning. Puppies instinctively whine and lick at their dam's muzzle to encourage her to regurgitate partially digested food for them. In this way they soon learn to associate whining with the arrival of food. Because it is based in instinct and strongly reinforced during weaning, begging can be tough to stop. Feeding bits of food to your dog from the dinner table only encourages begging—so don't do it!

Make Regular Health Checks

Every day, do a quick check for injuries, lumps, parasites, and skin irritations. Regardless of supervision, puppies find ingenious ways to hurt themselves. Rough play can cause muscle or tendon injuries. Chewing can result in a fractured tooth. Small wounds may not be immediately obvious. Similarly, ticks or fleas are easy to miss without a close inspection. Small changes in your puppy's personality or energy level can signal the onset of an illness. Poisoning and serious illnesses such as parvovirus (parvo) and distemper don't always begin with sudden drastic symptoms. Obvious changes in weight and eating habits at best may indicate a need for dietary revision and at worse signal possible illness.

Grooming

By the time she is three months old, your puppy should be familiar with basic grooming practices such as brushing, bathing (including blow-drying), ear cleaning, nail clipping, and teeth brushing. With persistence, most grooming routines can be mastered with a little practice and a lesson or two. Grooming instructions can be found in a multitude of books and videos. Many owners enjoy it, and it definitely helps to establish a bond with your puppy. In addition to its obvious role, grooming is a great way to alleviate tension (for both you and your puppy).

A well-trained Pembroke Welsh corgi sits quietly on a table as her fur is combed.

Train your puppy to stand on a table for grooming at home. It is far easier than trying to groom her on the floor or your lap, and your veterinarian and professional groomer will definitely appreciate this. Folding grooming tables are available from most pet supply companies. Or, have her stand on a nonskid mat placed on your kitchen table. For small puppies, a foam-backed placemat is perfect.

Brushing and Combing

Depending on coat type and lifestyle, regular brushing may be needed daily or weekly. Brushing removes dirt, improves circulation, and distributes natural oils through the coat (not to mention minimizes the amount of shed hair that clings to your clothes and furniture). Regular brushing removes tangles before they morph into mats and helps you notice fleas, ticks, or skin irritations before they become a serious problem. Some breeds experience extensive shedding when their coats start to lose their puppy textures and develop their adult looks, so frequent brushing is essential. In contrast to bathing, you really cannot brush your puppy too much, as long as you use the right tools and technique. Improperly done, brushing can cause skin irritations, coat damage, and a really bad attitude.

Always check for fleas and ticks when brushing. Fleas can be spotted crawling on the skin or by the telltale clue of "flea dirt"—bits of black grit in the coat. If you find a tick on your puppy, stay calm. Pull it off with tweezers or a tick remover. Do not apply gasoline or kerosene or attempt to burn it off. Once removed, destroy the tick before it locates a new victim—possibly you. If you suspect that a deer tick has bitten your puppy, you may want to have her tested for Lyme disease (if she hasn't already been vaccinated).

A wide-tooth metal comb is used to groom the coat of a Yorkshire terrier.

Bathing

Puppies usually need more frequent bathing than adult dogs do simply for aesthetic reasons—they get into all kinds of things. Cleanliness is important, but don't overdo it. Excessive bathing can upset the skin's normal pH balance, change texture, and remove a coat's oils. Daily combing or brushing goes a long way toward keeping a puppy clean. For most dogs, a bath once every week or two will do. Some breeds, though, should be bathed less frequently. For instance, too-frequent bathing of water retrievers will eliminate the natural oils that make their coats water repellent.

Puppies are more accepting of a bath if they are introduced to it by eight weeks of age. If not, a gradual acclimation can alleviate fear. Run the bath and test the water temperature before putting the puppy into the tub. The rinsing process generally gives rise to the most canine complaints. If your puppy begins to object, stop, reassure her, and wait until she calms down before you continue. Wrestling with an uncooperative dog is guaranteed to make matters worse. An agitated puppy can swallow water and choke, slip and fall, or jump out of the tub and injure herself. Don't underestimate how difficult it can be to get a grip on a wet, soapy puppy.

Before you begin, brush her coat to ensure it is free of mats and tangles. Once wet, it will be far more difficult to detangle, and tugging at the tangles will damage the hair. Additionally, the more hair you remove before she hits the tub, the less hair there will be to come off during the bath and clog the drain.

After a thorough brushing, place the puppy on a nonskid mat in the sink or bathtub. A hose attachment makes wetting and rinsing much easier. Otherwise, use a large pail or jug to pour warm (not hot!) water on her coat. Be careful when wetting her

A pair of lathered up golden retrievers await a good rinsing. It's important to get all the soap out; otherwise the dog's skin may be irritated or her coat damaged.

head not to get water in her ears or eyes. Water in the ears can lead to an infection, and water in the eyes is just plain uncomfortable; clean her face with a damp cloth. If you anticipate a lot of squirming or struggling, recruit a helper or restrain the puppy with a leash or grooming noose. Carefully apply shampoo, making sure not to get any into her eyes, nose, or mouth, and massage it all the way to the skin, paying special attention to legs, feet, belly, and tail. For short, thick coats, you may need to work against the hair growth to get the soap down to the skin. Don't use this method on a long coat—you'll create tangles! Starting from the head (not near the eyes!) and working down the neck to the back and sides to the tail, gently knead the soap through the coat from skin to hair tip. If the puppy is really dirty, you may need two applications of shampoo.

Rinse well. Failing to remove all the soap can cause skin irritations and coat damage. If you plan to apply a conditioner or rinse, have this premixed and ready. Some coat treatments must be left on for several minutes. Make sure the puppy does not become chilled or make a run for it. Have a good supply of bath towels at hand and perhaps a mop and a roll of paper towels.

Towel drying and shaking will remove a substantial amount of water from the coat. Even if the coat surface seems dry, it must be dry all the way to the skin or the puppy can become chilled. A hair dryer will speed up the process. If you plan to use a hair dryer regularly, put the puppy on a table and provide a small daily introduction until she feels comfortable. You may want to invest in a stand dryer or grooming arm and noose. This allows you to have two hands free to brush and style while drying.

Bath done, a golden allows herself to be blow-dried. For some dogs, you may need a stand dryer or a grooming arm and noose if you want to use a blow-dryer.

Nail Clipping

Puppy nails grow fast, and they are sharp. They can get caught in clothes or bedding, and the puppy may panic and end up with a broken nail. Nails should be trimmed every one to two weeks. When clipping a dog's nails, it is important not to hit the quick, a collection of blood vessels; cutting the quick will cause excessive bleeding. If a puppy's nails are kept short, the quick will recede, greatly reducing the possibility of clipping a nail too short. The quick is indicated by a pink line running down the middle of the nail, which may be difficult to spot in dogs with dark-colored nails. If you are not sure, just trim a tiny bit off each nail tip each week. The quick does not extend to the nail tip. After a few weeks, you will be able to estimate the proper amount to trim.

Holding the paw firmly, a woman clips the nails of her yellow Labrador retriever. You can purchase special puppy nail trimmers to do this job.

Hold the puppy on her back on your lap, or stand her on a nonskid surface and hold the foot pad up and begin. If the puppy objects to her pedicure, stay calm, tell her "no," ignore protests, and trim at least one more nail before you stop. You may need to trim just a few nails each day until she learns to accept this. Don't forget her dewclaws—the extra nails above her feet on her front legs. After trimming her nails, clip any excess hair that may be growing between the toes with a small, blunt-tipped scissors.

Regular nail clipping prevents an aversion to "foot phobia." It also helps owners overcome possible nervousness about attending to this chore. You may both need the practice. Puppy nail trimmers available from pet shops may be easier than models used on adult dogs. Some puppies (and owners) are more comfortable using a nail file or grinding tool.

An owner uses styptic powder on the paw of a Great Dane puppy to treat a bleeding nail.

Nail First Aid

IF YOU ACCIDENTALLY HIT THE QUICK, DON'T PANIC. *It looks far worse than it is. Use pressure to apply styptic powder to the nail to stop the bleeding. Other remedies include raking the nail across a bar of soap, packing it with flour to encourage clotting, or simply applying ice and pressure. Don't put it in water, as this will only slow the clotting. Don't let the puppy walk on the affected foot until you are sure the bleeding has stopped. Otherwise, the nail may start bleeding again, and you will be faced with the delightful prospect of cleaning bloody paw prints off everything.*

Dental Care

Good dental care is a combination of regular cleaning and inspection. Puppies use their mouths to investigate everything they find and can easily suffer cuts or burns to their mouths and

This bichon frise is being trained early to accept dental inspection and regular cleaning.

Plaque

DENTAL PLAQUE—A COMBINATION OF BACTERIA, WHITE blood cells, saliva, and food debris—accumulates on your puppy's teeth, but it can be easily removed. Hard food, dental chews, and regular cleaning will scrape off some debris. Daily or even weekly brushing will remove even more. If plaque is not removed, it will harden as it mixes with mineral deposits in saliva. This substance, tartar, cannot be removed by brushing. It will eventually work its way under the gum line, causing infections and destroying the tooth support. At that stage, bad breath will be accompanied by bleeding gums, loose teeth, and reluctance to chew. Treatment consists of cleaning and polishing, surgery to extract infected teeth, and antibiotic therapy to prevent the bacteria from damaging major organs.

tongues, or break teeth. A puppy's reluctance to have her mouth examined can be due to teething or an injury, but it could be a result of lack of training.

Even though a young puppy doesn't yet need professional teeth cleaning, this is the best time to train her to accept the process. Good dental care is important to health maintenance, and professional dental cleaning can cost between $100 and $250. It also carries the associated risk of putting the dog under anesthesia. It may not be possible to completely avoid professional cleaning, but the frequency can be minimized by regularly brushing your puppy's teeth at home.

Keep sessions short, and always end on a positive note, with praise and a treat. It may take as long as four weeks to train your puppy to cooperate. Plaque can be removed with a child's toothbrush, a doggy toothbrush, or a gauze pad wrapped around your finger. Experiment to find out which method works best for the size and shape of your puppy's mouth. Canine toothpaste is available from veterinarians and pet supply companies. Baking soda also works. Do not use human toothpaste. Dogs usually hate the taste, and it can cause stomach irritation. Brush the teeth in small circular motions, making sure to clean under the gum line.

Ear Cleaning

Any puppy can develop an ear infection or injury, but some breeds are more prone to accumulate earwax or develop yeast and fungal ear infections. Long, pendulous ears; narrow ear canals; or hair in ear canals are all contributing factors. Earflaps also attract burrs, fleas, and ticks. A puppy's ears are very sensitive, and minor infections or tiny injuries to ear leather (the inside flap of a dog ear) can be extremely painful. The puppy can make this worse by rubbing, scratching, and shaking the head. Without prompt treatment, this can lead to a painful hematoma of the earflap.

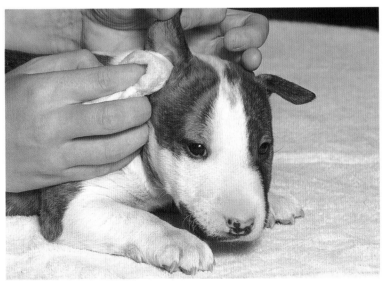

A bull terrier gets her ears gently, but thoroughly, cleaned. A puppy's ears can be easily infected, so always clean them during a regular grooming session.

Ear cleaning should be a part of your regular grooming routine. Squirt a few drops of ear cleaning solution into each ear, massage it well into the ear canal, and wipe away any moisture and earwax with a small piece of cotton. Do not probe deeply into the ear. A small amount of orange or yellow earwax is normal. Debris that is malodorous or is black, brown, or red can indicate ear mites or an infection. This will require a visit to your veterinarian for a definite diagnosis.

Excess hair can block airflow to the ear canals, provide a conduit for bacteria, and promote wax buildup. Removing excess hair growth from the ear canals should be a regular part of ear cleaning. You can trim the hair with blunt-tipped scissors, but plucking is the best method. Sprinkle a small bit of ear powder into the canal, and grasp and pull out a few hairs with your fingertips, tweezers, or a hemostat. Don't pull too much at once. Swab out the ear with cleaning solution afterward.

With cotton, an owner carefully cleans around the eyes of her puppy.

Anal Glands

ALL DOGS MUST HAVE THEIR ANAL GLANDS EMPTIED regularly. The anal glands are two grape-size sacs located on the sides of the anus. These fluid-filled glands usually release their contents naturally when the dog eliminates, leaving behind her scent. Sometimes the fluid is not released, which over time causes the glands to become swollen and emit a foul odor. If a dog's anal glands are swollen, she will probably scoot her bottom along the ground in an effort to relieve the pressure. If you notice this behavior, you should manually empty the glands for her. (Most groomers will perform this for you, usually for an extra fee. Have your groomer check the status of the glands at each visit.) If neglected, anal glands can become impacted, infected, or abscessed. Manually expressing the glands is not complicated or painful, but a puppy can be frightened if not familiarized with the procedure. Hold up the puppy's tail and gently squeeze the anal area between your thumb and forefinger. Do this outdoors, or preferably with the puppy in a bathtub. Aim the puppy away from you! The fluid is extremely foul smelling, and it can shoot out with surprising speed and force when the glands are squeezed. The odor is difficult to remove. Normally, the expelled liquid is watery and brownish. If the glands are impacted, it will be thick and tarlike. Expressing impacted glands requires a trip to the vet.

Finding a Groomer

All dogs need regular grooming. Be realistic about how much grooming you are willing or able to manage. If your puppy has a high-maintenance coat or requires a special cut, you will need to find a professional dog groomer. Expertise includes more than hair styling. An expert groomer is skilled at spotting little things that you might not notice, such as small injuries, parasites, suspicious lumps, or unusual behavior. The groomer can also be an excellent source for care and training advice.

Groomers can vary drastically in their skills, credentials, and fees. Ask local veterinarians and dog trainers for recommendations. Do some comparison shopping, and don't hesitate to drop in to look around before making a choice. Visits to a groomer can be wonderful opportunities for puppy training and socialization—but they can also be traumatizing experiences and opportunities to pick up fleas or kennel cough.

Does the establishment look and smell clean? Is the equipment clean, new, and of high quality? Do the dogs seem calm and happy? A chaotic environment is not likely to enhance your puppy's social skills. How about the staff? A trip to the grooming shop should be comparable to a visit for you to a beauty spa. Your puppy should eagerly anticipate the visit and return looking and feeling wonderful. Are the security precautions adequate to ensure that dogs cannot escape or be accidentally injured? What are the procedures for handling emergencies? Are all pets required to have proof of vaccination?

Ask what services are included in a regular grooming session. Does the shop charge extra for nail clipping, expressing anal glands, or cleaning ears? Are the dogs placed in cage dryers after bathing? If so, make sure that this is supervised. If the shop offers pick up and delivery services, find out who actually does this. Does it offer other services, such as day care, pet sitting, dog walking, or training? Is it difficult to get an appointment? Are you required to leave your puppy for an entire day?

Daily Exercise Routine

A puppy needs more exercise than an adult dog does. Overdoing it can stress developing joints, but limiting a puppy's exercise can be far more damaging. The effects of degenerative joint disease

A weimaraner pup gets plenty of exercise and fresh air as she runs across a field. Exercise should be a regular part of every puppy's daily activities.

can be minimized by good muscle development. For fragile breeds, exercise will build bone density and decrease risk of fractures. Large or small, a puppy will never learn how to jump, fall, or land safely without practice.

A puppy's exercise routine must be tailored to her metabolic demands, which are largely determined by her breed. One intensive workout may fit better into your daily schedule, but it probably won't work for a puppy, mentally or physically. Plan on short, frequent sessions. This may require hiring a dog walker or joining a puppy day care program.

A dog's motivation to exercise varies regardless of the need for activity. Don't assume that your puppy is diligently jogging around the yard simply because you put her out there. Plan to devote daily time to your puppy's exercise. Taking your puppy for a walk or playing with her contributes tremendously to bonding and socialization.

6

Your Puppy's Health

A golden retriever munches on his ball toy. Obsessive chewing may be a sign of teething.

Y OUR PUPPY'S HEALTH IS A PRIMARY RESPONSIBILITY OF dog ownership. That doesn't imply that it needs to be a constant source of worry. If you have done your homework and selected a healthy puppy and take proper care of him, your trips to the veterinarian will be fewer. To a great extent, keeping your puppy healthy involves nothing more than sensible maintenance and familiarity with your puppy's normal mental and physical state. This ensures that you will recognize and treat minor problems before they evolve into major health issues.

Teething

Teething starts around four months of age and usually leads to obsessive chewing. Some puppies will have no interest in chewing and may not even want to eat because of inflamed gums or fever. The eruption of the canines and molars usually cause the most pain. In rare cases, teething may be accompanied by a sinus or lymph node infection, with swelling under the eyes or around the jaw or neck. If teething causes your puppy obvious discomfort, you should consult your veterinarian. Although this is a temporary phase, the doctor may have suggestions for minimizing the associated pain.

Normal Teeth Growth

YOUR PUPPY'S FORTY-TWO PERMANENT TEETH WILL erupt in the following sequence:

4–5 months: incisor 1, incisor 2, incisor 3, premolar 1, molar 1

5–6 months: canines, premolar 2, premolar 3, premolar 4, molar 2

6–7 months: molar 3

Normally, the bud for each permanent tooth is aligned directly under the primary tooth it is destined to replace. As it begins to erupt, the adult tooth absorbs the calcium and the root of its predecessor. Give the puppy plenty of chew toys and regularly check to see if the puppy tooth is loosening. If it shows no indications of vacating the premises, consult your veterinarian and arrange to have it extracted.

Retained baby teeth can cause crowding, crooked teeth, and dental decay. One crooked tooth can trigger a "domino effect" resulting in permanent misalignment of the bite. If a retained tooth is causing a problem, it's best to have it removed. Extraction does not require a specialist in canine dentistry. The procedure does require anesthesia, but it can be done at your regular veterinarian's office. Puppy teeth are thin and brittle and must be removed carefully to avoid damaging the permanent tooth buds underneath.

Puppy Vaccinations

The primary source of a newborn puppy's immunity is colostrum, the dam's initial milk secretions, which are high in protein and antibody content. Even though antibodies cannot be absorbed into the bloodstream after the first twenty-four hours, puppies will continue to receive immune protection as long as they are nursing. Immunoglobulin G and A in the milk continue to provide protection against infections of the mouth, digestive system, and intestinal mucous membranes—the most common routes of infection. This is one reason a puppy should remain

A trio of bloodhounds snuggle on a sofa. A puppy's initial immunity comes from the mother's milk, so the pup should not be separated from his mother until he's at least eight weeks old.

with his dam until at least eight weeks of age. This immunity is natural, safe, and extremely effective, but temporary. Eventually, it must be replaced by vaccinations.

Vaccines

IN RECENT YEARS, THE SAFETY AND EFFECTIVENESS OF canine vaccines have become a subject of debate. There are valid concerns, but they should not serve to downplay the risks of diseases.

All puppies should be vaccinated against distemper, parvovirus, adenovirus, and rabies. Puppy vaccinations are usually administered in one combined dose, known as DHLPP: distemper, hepatitis (adenovirus type 1), Leptospira, parvovirus, and parainfluenza. Many vaccines are available with variations of these components. The DHLPP vaccination is a three-dosage series, with the first shot usually administered between six and eight weeks of age, the second at about twelve weeks of age, and the third at about sixteen weeks of age. A rabies vaccination should always be given separately, usually at four months of age, and followed up one year later; a rabies booster is generally recommended every three years afterward. If you live in a rural area or will be walking your puppy in woodsy grounds where ticks are prevalent, your veterinarian may recommend vaccinating against Lyme disease.

Immunity acquired from the dam begins to wane by six to eight weeks of age and usually disappears by twelve to sixteen weeks. Normally, the puppy's immune system begins to function by then to compensate. *Vaccinations will not be effective until the puppy's immune system is fully functional.* Vaccinations given earlier than eight weeks of age are more likely to interfere with, rather than stimulate, an immune response.

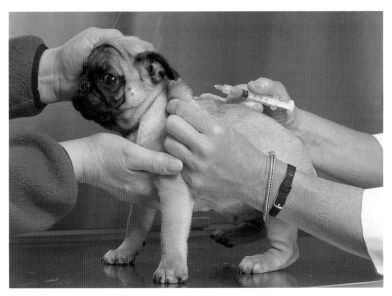

A nervous-looking pug receives a vaccination. The vet has pinched up a layer of skin into which she will insert the needle.

The same vaccination schedule is not appropriate for every pup. A veterinarian may wait to administer vaccinations until the puppy has reached a certain weight, regardless of the dog's age. Similarly, which vaccinations are necessary can depend on where you live, what kinds of activities your dog participates in, and your dog's breed. Certain diseases, for instance, pose a greater risk in some areas of the country than in others. Puppies who are exposed to wild animals or other dogs on a regular basis (at dog shows or kennels, for instance) require more extensive protection than a puppy who rarely leaves his home turf. Large and small breeds have different needs and drug sensitivities.

Deworming

Most commonly, puppies harbor roundworms or hookworms. Ingesting eggs from a contaminated environment is the most common source of infection. A puppy can also acquire either one from his dam. If the dam has ever been infected, she can transmit this to her puppies through dormant larvae during pregnancy or from nursing. Both of these parasites can be transmitted to humans. Most commonly, this happens to children who fail to wash their hands after playing in the dirt, where parasite eggs have been shed in the feces of infected dogs. Eating with unwashed hands, the children can end up ingesting the parasite eggs.

In dogs, roundworms can cause severe diarrhea, lower immunity, cause intestinal blockages, and migrate to the eye, liver, or lungs, causing secondary bacterial pneumonia. Diarrhea is also the main symptom of hookworm. Bloody diarrhea can lead to anemia

Microchipping

IMPLANTING AN ID MICROCHIP, WHICH IS THE SIZE OF A grain of rice and contains a unique identity code, is comparable to administering a vaccination. Although the microchip needle is large, most puppies tolerate it well. Microchips are implanted under the skin between the shoulders. One chip will last for a lifetime, but sometimes a chip will migrate to another part of the body, and a scanner won't pick up the code. In that case, the chip must be replaced. Some of the newer microchip designs have been reconfigured to prevent them from migrating. Ask your veterinarian. The placement of the chip can be verified during your dog's annual checkup.

Fees to implant the microchip can range from $30 to $75. An additional fee may be charged for registration. It is important to register the chip because the microchip number and your contact information are not automatically entered into the company's database. Although microchipping is a reliable means of permanent identification, it does not guarantee recovery of your puppy if he is lost or stolen. It certainly raises the odds, but it also depends on factors beyond your control. An old-fashioned ID tag attached to the collar is a good backup.

and secondary infections as a result of compromised immune function. Checking a fecal sample for the presence of parasites is normally a part of your puppy's first veterinary visit. The doctor will advise you when the puppy should be checked again.

Regardless of what type of parasites you are dealing with, deworming will not be effective unless you discover the source of the problem and stop the cycle of infestation. Sources can range from contaminated soil or water to contact with infected wild or stray animals.

Spaying and Neutering

If you don't plan to breed or show your puppy, neutering decreases risks of diseases, such as testicular and mammary cancers and ovarian and uterine disease; prevents the possibility of an unwanted litter; and can help you manage behavior problems. The surgery is generally safe, and most puppies are back in action within a day. Some veterinarians require an overnight stay; others will send the puppies home after they awaken from the anesthesia. Some techniques use dissolvable sutures, and others use standard sutures that will need to be removed.

For very large or very small breeds, many dog professionals recommend waiting until the puppy has achieved full adult growth before spaying or neutering. For large breeds, waiting will ensure complete bone growth. For small breeds, it reduces the risks associated with surgery under anesthesia. But most dogs can be altered as early as eight weeks of age.

First Aid

Every puppy owner should become familiar with basic first aid procedures and keep a first aid manual and an emergency medical kit on hand. Keep them in one place. You will not want to be dashing around the house searching for medical supplies in an emergency. If your puppy becomes suddenly ill or is injured, remain calm and methodically evaluate his condition so you can take the appropriate measures. The most serious life-threatening emergencies are respiratory arrest, circulatory collapse, shock, and severe bleeding, all of which can be fatal long before you arrive at the veterinary hospital. Be sure to ask your regular veterinarian about the clinic's emergency hours and whether they have a special emergency telephone number. You may also want to map the route to the nearest emergency animal hospital. Consider enrolling in an emergency first aid course for pets. For more information, visit http://www.redcross.org/services/disaster/beprepared/firstaid.html.

Injuries

No matter how carefully you puppy proof your home and yard and supervise your dog, accidents happen. The important thing is to be prepared and to act calmly and quickly. Never forcefully handle a severely injured puppy; you can cause further injury. Never lift or move an injured body part without supporting it. You can construct a makeshift splint from a ruler or rolled up newspaper. If the puppy is unconscious, place him on a board to prevent possible back or neck damage. If he is agitated due to pain, disorientation, or seizures, put him in a crate to prevent further injury. A puppy is not in any danger of swallowing his tongue during a seizure, but he can break a bone or give himself a concussion by falling or thrashing around.

If the puppy feels cool when you place your hand against the skin on flank or stomach, wrap him in a blanket to prevent

Your Puppy's First Aid Kit

THE FOLLOWING PRODUCTS ARE AVAILABLE IN MOST drug stores. Consult your veterinarian about the proper dosage of any medication for your puppy's age and weight.

- Assorted sterile bandages and dressing
- Benadryl to counteract allergic reactions
- Blankets and towels
- Disinfectant solution for flushing out wounds (Betadine or Nolvasan)
- First aid tape
- Hot and cold packs
- Ointments for minor wounds and skin irritations (cortisone ointment, first aid cream)
- Oral glucose solution and syringe or eyedropper to administer dosage
- Over-the-counter medications for vomiting and diarrhea
- Pediatric glucose solution
- Penlight or tiny flashlight
- Peroxide
- Phone numbers of your veterinarian, closest emergency clinic, and poison control center
- Rolls of gauze (can also be used for makeshift muzzle)
- Rubbing alcohol
- Scissors (large and small blunt-tipped, bandage scissors)
- Self-sticking bandages
- Splinting materials (depending on the size of the puppy, this may be a plastic spoon, paint stick, ruler, or ideally, a foam-padded plastic splint)
- Sterile cotton
- Sterile eye wash or artificial tears
- Stethoscope
- Styptic powder or styptic pencil to stop minor bleeding
- Thermometer
- Tweezers

A bichon endures the process of having his temperature taken. If you have never used a rectal thermometer on a pet before, ask your vet for tips.

loss of body heat. This is a sign of potentially fatal shock. Provide extra warmth with a heat pack or hot-water bottle; make sure it is warm, not hot, and do not place it directly against the puppy's skin; wrapping the heat pack in a thin towel will help prevent burning of his skin while allowing the pack to heat the body. Conversely, if the puppy is overheated, wrap him in cool, wet towels and cold packs to lower his body temperature. Never give water or medications to an unconscious puppy. He will not be able to swallow and may choke or aspirate fluids into his lungs.

Airway Obstruction

Choking, gagging, pawing at the mouth, facial contortions, blue color of the lips and tongue, or noisy or exaggerated breathing indicate that the puppy's airway is obstructed. Struggling or gasping can cause a partially obstructed airway to become totally blocked and can lead to suffocation.

If the puppy is choking on something he has swallowed, try to dislodge it with a finger sweep. This must be done carefully to avoid possibly lodging it more firmly and causing a total obstruction. Do not elevate the puppy's head or lay him on his back. Open his mouth, and pull the tongue forward. Fully extend the neck, and insert an index finger into the mouth. Use a hooking motion to probe down the insides of his cheeks and into the back of his throat. If you feel the object, carefully extract it.

If you cannot locate the obstruction, you can attempt five to ten abdominal thrust compressions, similar to the Heimlich maneuver. Stand the puppy on all four feet, keeping his head lowered. Grasp him firmly around his middle, just below the rib cage, and compress his abdomen quickly and firmly to dislodge the obstruction.

Immediately transport the puppy to the veterinarian, keeping him in a horizontal position. Elevating the head will decrease blood flow to the brain and may trigger cardiac arrest. Even if the puppy regains consciousness, you may need to perform artificial respiration.

Artificial Respiration

Lack of spontaneous breathing can be caused by electrocution, suffocation, obstruction, head trauma, or drowning. The puppy's gums, lips, and tongue will turn blue, and his pupils may become dilated. If his lungs are full of fluid, hold him upside down and compress his sides to remove the fluid before starting artificial respiration. Clean away all mucus, saliva, and vomit.

Extend the puppy's neck and pull the tongue forward. Close the jaws over the tongue, and breathe twelve to twenty breaths into the puppy's nostrils (a puppy under five pounds may

A Great Dane pup gets his weight taken with the use of a light plastic basket and a small scale. Part of keeping track of your pet's health is keeping track of his weight losses and gains.

need up to thirty breaths per minute). Make sure the puppy's lips are tightly closed so air is directed into his lungs. Don't do this too forcefully, or you can rupture lung tissue. The chest cavity should expand with each breath.

Cardiac Chest Compressions

Shock, drowning, electrocution, and severe trauma can cause a puppy's heart to stop beating. Check for a heartbeat by placing your hand along his rib cage slightly behind the breastbone. Or, check his pulse by placing your fingers on the large artery on the inside of the thigh.

If you cannot detect a pulse or heartbeat and the puppy does not respond to artificial respiration, start chest compressions to get oxygen circulating through the body and stimulate the heart to start beating. If you do not have assistance, give two breaths of artificial respiration after every fifteen chest compressions. Do not attempt to do chest compressions if the puppy has broken ribs.

For a large puppy, lay him on his right side and use the palm of your hand to compress the side of the rib cage, approximately at the point of the elbow. For a very small puppy, place him on his back and compress the sides of the rib cage with your thumb and forefinger. Depress the rib cage 1.5 to 3 inches, 80 to 140 times per minute. The smaller the puppy, the greater the chest compression rate needed. Continue this for at least fifteen minutes or until spontaneous breathing and heartbeat have been reestablished.

Treating Shock

Shock (complete cardiovascular collapse) can result from trauma, electrocution, bleeding, infection, dehydration, or heatstroke. Signs include weak heartbeat; rapid pulse; shallow breathing; pale gray or white lips, gums, and tongue; low body temperature; weakness; and unconsciousness.

Capillary refill time (CRT) can indicate evidence of shock. Apply pressure to the puppy's gum tissue. Normally, it is a pale pink, and this color should return within one second (the CRT) of removing your finger. If the gum tissue remains pale for more than two seconds, the puppy may be in shock.

Shock will be fatal if not reversed. Gradually warm the puppy to raise his body temperature by wrapping his body in blankets. A heat pack or hot-water bottle can also be used, but first wrap it in a thin towel to avoid overheating the skin surface, which can make matters worse. If the puppy is responsive and strong enough to drink, give him an oral pediatric glucose solution. This may prevent the condition from worsening until he can receive IV fluids at the veterinary hospital.

Bleeding

If a major vein or artery has been nicked or severed, this can cause shock, circulatory collapse, and fatal damage to major organs within minutes. Clean the wound to find the source and degree of injury. Maintain firm pressure over the wound with a cloth, a gauze pad, or even a towel or T-shirt. This is more effective and less risky than applying a tourniquet. Transport the puppy to a vet as soon as the bleeding is under control. The puppy may require IV fluids, a transfusion, or stitches.

Poisoning

Puppies are at risk for poisoning due to their arbitrary eating habits. They can also be poisoned in less obvious ways, such as by having reactions to prescription medications or flea control products, inhaling fumes, receiving bites from reptiles or insects, or absorbing poisonous substances through the skin.

Amounts of a potentially toxic substance that would not cause illness in an adult dog can be fatal to a small puppy. Some common substances that cause poisoning in a puppy include acetaminophen, antifreeze, chocolate, flea control products, ivermectin, rodent poisons, snail bait, household plants, garden herbicides, and insecticides.

Symptoms can range from vomiting and diarrhea, drooling, ulceration of the mouth and throat, swelling of the tongue, disorientation, staggering, or convulsions, depending on the type

A veterinarian gives a Saint Bernard puppy a thorough exam. Take your pet to the vet for regular exams and at the first sign of serious illness.

of poison ingested. Call the ASPCA Animal Poison Control Center (formerly the National Animal Poison Control Center) at 1-888-426-4435. (Have a credit card ready; you may be billed $55 as a consultation fee.) If you know exactly what toxic substance your puppy has consumed, you may be advised to induce vomiting by administering 3 percent hydrogen peroxide. If you suspect that your puppy has been poisoned, but you don't know what he has ingested, do not induce vomiting. If a caustic substance was ingested, vomiting can worsen the problem. Regardless of the amount of toxic substance ingested, transport your puppy to the veterinarian immediately.

7

Your
Growing Puppy

These American Staffordshire terriers, like all puppies, will go through several distinctive development stages on the road to adulthood.

WATCHING NEWBORN PUPPIES GROW AND CHANGE IS something you never tire of. During their earliest weeks, their behavior is orchestrated by intricate reflexes, refined to perfection in their ancient canine ancestors. Nothing is left to chance. As they grow, their behavior is continually revised to get the most out of their improving life skills. Behavioral changes can be traced to internal changes as well as external influences. For instance, once a puppy possesses a good set of choppers, she begins to chew and bite anything that comes her way. This new behavior is quickly modified when she decides to test out her new teeth on her mom or siblings.

There is no consensus about exactly when a puppy's personality stabilizes. Many aspects of personality, such as a

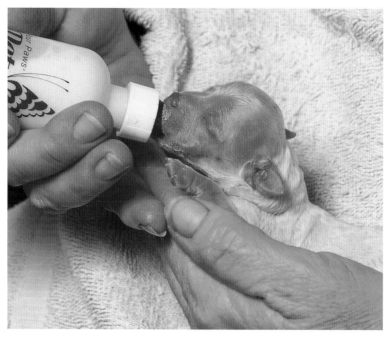

A newborn bichon sucks from a bottle. Ideally, a pup this young should be fed by her mother, which helps establish the dog-to-dog socialization bond.

propensity for aggression, do not become clearly established until adulthood. Depending on the breed, this delay may vary from twelve months to three years of age.

Why Is Socialization So Important?

Socialization is one of the most demanding aspects of raising a puppy and one of the most important. Like all animals, dogs are naturally wary of anything unfamiliar. This is essential to survival. Of course, understanding the environment is equally essential to survival. Puppies must absorb a tremendous amount of information during their early weeks. They are highly impressionable, and every new experience counts.

Dog-to-Dog Socialization

A puppy's first social contact takes place with her mother. Even though the bonding between a mother and her pup begins at birth, this is a learned behavior, triggered by smell and touch, a puppy's only well-developed senses at birth. This bond enables a puppy to recognize her mother, her species, and her breed. Puppies are genetically programmed to socialize with other dogs and will try to do this as soon as they can walk, generally at three or four weeks old. They need regular contact with other dogs until they are at least six weeks old.

In addition, dogs are extremely perceptive about recognizing specific individuals but don't automatically extend this to the rest of the species, especially if a puppy's canine socialization has been limited to just one other dog or only one breed. A cocker spaniel might have no trouble recognizing a field spaniel, but a greyhound might not receive an automatic welcome. A small dog who has been raised exclusively with large dogs can develop a fear of dogs her own size. And a puppy may be comfortable with well-known humans and pets and still act shy when faced with a stranger—or even with a well-known person who appears wearing some unfamiliar article of clothing. Depending on a puppy's natural temperament, the familiarization process may necessitate gradual, individualized introductions to all sorts of unusual things.

Breeders provide puppies with opportunities to interact with dogs and humans as soon as the critical time of contact commences. Otherwise, a puppy may always have trouble relating to other dogs. She may overreact or behave timidly when meeting other dogs and is more likely to be fearful or aggressive. Poor socialization will also affect her ability to relate to humans.

A golden retriever and a duckling become acquainted. If you have animals of other species, you'll want to make sure your puppy knows they're fellow residents—not lunch.

Socialization Toward Other Species

Part of the socialization process includes learning to accept unfamiliar individuals. A puppy can easily bond with any species until about four months of age. If you don't want your puppy to chase cats or kill chickens, socialization toward other species during these months can prevent it. This may be a major concern for breeds with a high predatory drive (such as Rhodesian ridgebacks, greyhounds, and border terriers) who will be expected to cohabit with other household pets. Make sure your puppy has regular interaction with other species from as early an age as possible. This will help to modify normal predator/prey relationships into social attachments.

Socialization Toward People

A puppy needs both human and canine socialization. Without adequate human contact, she will prefer dogs to humans. She will tolerate people but not trust them or form close attachments. This makes the puppy less responsive to training because she has little motivation to communicate and bond with humans.

Puppies vary in the amount of experience they need to become socialized to people. This is due to a combination of individual temperament, environment, and genetics. Some can become well socialized with twenty minutes of interaction twice a week. For timid puppies or breeds who are naturally aloof, such as pharaoh hounds and basenjis, this can be completely inadequate. Such breeds will probably need daily interaction throughout their spontaneous socialization period as well as regular reinforcement of these lessons until adulthood.

This Pembroke Welsh corgi enjoys some one-on-one time. Breeders give puppies without any littermates a good deal of personal attention to help with socialization.

The Motivation to Socialize

Every puppy's attitude toward the entire meet-and-greet process differs. An outgoing, confident puppy will be more inclined to socialize. For some breeds, the desire to interact and socialize has been discouraged through either natural or artificial selection. For instance, primitive breeds (breeds thought to have changed little from their ancestors) and guardian breeds, such as Thai Ridgebacks, Tibetan mastiffs, and cane corsos, are naturally wary. But even difficult cases can and do become well socialized if you are willing to take the time to work with them. The success of this process depends on the puppy's ability to dismiss her natural fear; so, initial introductions should not be too forceful.

A young boy offers his rottweiler a refreshing drink of water. Interacting with people and other animals is especially important for a puppy during the first weeks of life.

Littermates and Social Attachment

LIMITED SOCIAL ATTACHMENT CAN OCCUR IF TWO *littermates are raised together. If this becomes the primary source of their social interaction, they may become extremely bonded and reluctant to interact with anyone else. They will also exhibit intense anxiety if separated. It is certainly possible to successfully raise canine littermates. But they must have regular opportunities to learn, grow, and socialize individually.*

How well a puppy is socialized also depends on the owner's attitude. A puppy can suppress her desire to socialize if this is the message you impart. In general, the more intense an attachment a puppy forms to one individual, the less motivated she will be to form other relationships. Excessive nurturing can interfere with a puppy's socialization, and she may become obsessively focused on human attention to the exclusion of everything else. This can happen when an overprotective owner insulates a puppy from the environment. Such an owner may not permit the puppy to go out, socialize, or play with other dogs, fearing that she may be frightened, be injured, or contract some illness.

Generally, the socialization period begins to wane when a puppy reaches twelve weeks of age, largely due to developing memory and establishing connections between themselves (their behaviors) and the environment. For instance, puppies learn that some things should be feared or avoided. A degree of natural wariness is a survival skill, a legacy of their wolf heritage. Domesticated dogs experience this uneasiness later in life and to a lesser degree than their wolf ancestors, but it remains part of their makeup. Socialization must begin as early as possible; the longer you wait, the less accepting your puppy will be of new experiences and new faces.

Doberman pinscher littermates share a meal. Puppies exposed to only their littermates can become extremely bonded, which will be detrimental to other relationships.

Playing and Learning

Contented dogs of all ages are prone to spontaneous outbursts of playfulness. Playing is strongly linked to socialization and a sense of security. Well-socialized dogs never completely outgrow their interest in playing, whereas poorly socialized dogs may never feel confident enough to indulge. They may actually perceive normal play gestures as threatening, responding to them with fear or with aggression.

There is no doubt that puppies relish play, but playing is also a form of learning. Through it, a puppy hones the physical and mental skills she will need to survive. In addition to perfecting survival skills, playing facilitates exercise, social interaction, and the opportunity to assess the behavior of others.

Investigative Play

A puppy begins to investigate her environment as soon as she leaves her whelping box. Investigative play is more than juvenile entertainment—it is a genetically determined imperative. This is how a puppy learns to understand her environment. Although it is natural to discourage a puppy from getting into things, this is a mistake. Overprotecting a puppy during these weeks may shield her from potential dangers, but caution must be balanced with an effort to maximize her learning potential. She will never regain this amazing capacity to absorb new information.

Interactive Play

All the complicated social skills a puppy will need as an adult must be learned. Her earliest lessons come from her dam, during play. After the puppy's primary teeth erupt, the mother becomes

The interesting aromas from a can of garbage capture a rottweiler's attention. Don't be too quick to discourage a puppy from learning about the world—not until she starts tossing the garbage around.

By playing with an adult dog, this puppy learns what is acceptable, and what is not, in her interactions with other dogs.

less willing to tolerate nursing or rough play. Puppies don't automatically pay attention to these warnings, and the dam will growl or snap to emphasize her message.

These lessons are reinforced when the puppy plays with other dogs, usually in the form of stalking, chasing, sparring, and roughhousing. These play sessions may seem savage, but they provide a vital outlet for canine predatory energy and a means of learning the limits of acceptable behavior and the warning signs leading up to them. Play fighting teaches a puppy the connection between biting and pain. This is how a puppy learns to curb the intensity of her bites and threats. Dogs possess enormous control over their bite power, but this is learned.

Puppies will not hesitate to initiate play fights with adult dogs, and many adults will join in the fun, patiently enduring attention from puppies that they would never tolerate from another adult dog. Some adults, however, have absolutely no sympathy for puppies. Never assume that a dog is going to be patient or friendly when confronted by an unruly puppy. And even a patient dog's tolerance will steadily decline as a puppy matures. Rough or socially inept behavior will eventually receive a nasty response. Of course, by that time, a puppy has usually learned to control her behavior thanks to interactive play.

Playing with Humans

Most dogs are highly motivated to play with humans because they find it so rewarding. Playing with your puppy is far more than a recreational pastime; it is one of the easiest ways to establish trust and communication with a new puppy, and it provides her with the opportunity to expend her excess mental and physical energy in acceptable ways.

Just as they do with other dogs, puppies will "test the waters" to learn exactly how far they can go with you before getting into trouble. Interactive games are a great way for you to redirect unacceptable forms of play through clear, consistent feedback. No nipping, jumping up, or chasing people. The fact that dogs play roughly with each other is no reason to tolerate this behavior when your puppy plays with you. This may not seem like a big deal when she is small, but it would become a major issue when she is a full-grown dog with adult-size teeth and adult-strength jaw power.

Problems that arise during human-canine play are not due to the form of play but to a failure to set boundaries and understand canine gestures. As a puppy matures, she will begin to display adult behaviors relating to pack status and territoriality during play. Don't assume that this cannot become a problem just because it happens during play. Puppies also have short attention spans. Their perceptions and intentions can shift in the midst of

Playing fetch with this golden retriever is not only good exercise but also a way for the dog to learn appropriate behavior with people.

a play session. If you fail to react appropriately, this reinforces message that it's OK to challenge humans.

Other dogs routinely discourage a puppy's aggressive play and hard biting. Bite inhibition that a puppy learns from canine contacts is not necessarily carried over to human encounters. If the puppy bites, stop the game immediately. Loudly announce your injury to the puppy with an emphatic "ouch!" If necessary, hold the puppy's muzzle while doing this. The puppy will understand that the bite caused you to hurt. Stop playing and ignore the puppy for a few minutes. She may want to immediately resume playing. Don't give in.

Pack Mentality

Pack mentality no longer plays a role in canine survival, but it still significantly affects a puppy's growth and development, influencing her evolving personality. As she observes and interacts with members of your household, your puppy gradually comes to understand how and where she fits in. A young puppy will be content to occupy a low-ranking position. She becomes much more concerned with her rank when she enters adolescence.

A puppy's understanding of her role in the pack can impart a sense of security, lessen anxiety, and curb extreme personality tendencies. Unlike people, dogs have no desire for independence. Their contentment is contingent on maintaining a state of emotional dependence. A puppy can occupy a subordinate role within her pack with no loss of confidence or happiness. This is true regardless of whether she has a dominant or submissive temperament.

An American Eskimo puppy runs after an adult pack mate. Puppies learn their places in the pack as they grow and interact with the other dogs.

A consistent environment makes the puppy understand her particular role in your pack. This is why it is so important to adhere to a regular routine and to be consistent when communicating with your puppy. If a puppy senses that order is lacking, she may attempt to create it. This can mean implementing her own "pack rules" in your household.

Challenging the Status Quo

Approaching maturity encourages many adolescent puppies to attempt some challenge to authority. A clear understanding of rules and boundaries is no guarantee that your puppy won't try to revise them. This does not imply that your puppy has some sort of devious, takeover agenda. She is merely doing what comes naturally.

From a canine's point of view, social interaction is an ongoing invitation to improve one's standing in the pack. If the opportunity arises, a puppy will attempt to manipulate relationships with humans. Your reaction will let her know whether it's safe to continue. Be firm and consistent.

Timeline for Trouble

THE FOLLOWING ARE ALL NORMAL, INSTINCTIVE CANINE behaviors that can lead to conflicts over rank and dominance. Although they work perfectly well in a canine pack, they are bound to lead to problems in a human household. At best, they can make your puppy difficult to live with. At worst, they can lead to aggressive confrontations of some form.

- Five weeks: a puppy may begin guarding food.
- Two months: play fighting can take on overtones of real aggression.
- Three months: territorial guarding can emerge.
- Four or five months: a puppy can begin to show defensive aggression by nipping or growling to avoid something the puppy does not want to do, such as being bathed or meeting a dog or person she doesn't want to socialize with.

Simply recognizing and discouraging these behaviors as they arise is usually sufficient to nip any potential problem in the bud. It's up to you to let the puppy know what is OK and what is not.

Adolescent Behaviors

Regardless of sex, breed, or background, preadolescence triggers hormonal changes. The adrenal gland produces testosterone in both sexes. Male puppies are especially prone to erratic behavior around four to five months of age when their testosterone levels begin to rise.

A puppy may resort to barking, howling, digging, and chewing simply to relieve boredom and frustration. Some breeds are more energetic than others, but every puppy needs a daily outlet for mental and physical energy. If you don't provide this, she will find her own. Much of this behavior is self-rewarding, so habits form effortlessly.

Surgery

Neutering (male dog) or spaying (female dog) can be an effective remedy for many behavior problems, but it is not an absolute preventive for anything except breeding. The procedure will not transform a poorly socialized or badly trained puppy into a model pet. Although neutering will curb a male's threshold for aggression, as testosterone levels become lower, a puppy accustomed to getting away with aggression or bullying is not likely to change unless neutering is combined with behavior modification. Fearful aggression will not diminish after neutering because it is not hormonal in origin. Spaying will not reduce dominant aggression in females; in fact, it may have the opposite effect on a naturally dominant female.

Mounting and territorial leg lifting can be difficult to discourage in either sex after they have become established habits. They are a combination of instinct and bad habits, so neutering will have no effect. It is also unlikely to counteract destructive behavior. These are neurotic responses to anxiety, boredom, and loneliness. The onset of adolescence may intensify these problems simply because the puppy is bigger and capable of doing more damage.

Shyness

Breeds who are prone to natural wariness, such as the komondor and the Neopolitan mastiff, may become noticeably shy during adolescence when guardian instincts begin to emerge. These breeds are not recommended for inexperienced dog owners who might not be able to recognize or manage this behavior, which may include suspicion toward strangers, protectiveness toward family members, territoriality, and displays of aggression. A formerly friendly puppy may become reluctant to socialize. Giving in to this attitude will encourage antisocial tendencies.

This komondor and her pups are naturally wary. The puppies may become even shier when they become adolescents.

Shyness may also be an adolescent response to limited early socialization. As the puppy matures, she becomes less able to cope with the stress of social encounters and becomes reluctant to meet strangers or visit unfamiliar places. Forcing the puppy into uncomfortable encounters can make matters worse. Instinctive fight-or-flight decisions may be her only choices.

Dominance

During adolescence, a dominant puppy may begin to bully other pets by guarding her food, toys, or bed. Or, she may attempt to dominate human members of the household through aggression or by disobeying rules. Tolerating this behavior will be seen as an invitation to continue. Dominant puppies are usually content as long as they get what they want. However, they are not in the habit of backing down when they don't.

Dog Aggression

It's not unusual for conflicts to arise between formerly congenial dogs when a puppy reaches adolescence. Most commonly, hostility develops between dogs living in the same house. As a puppy matures, she may challenge other dogs as she tries to improve her ranking in the pack, thus provoking confrontations.

A dog's rank in a household pack results from ongoing dominant and submissive interactions between canine *and* human pack members. One dog in the household is usually known as the "alpha," or highest ranking, dog, which minimizes possible confrontations. If the dogs are peaceful, the alpha dog should be allowed all the privileges of her status. Dogfights can be triggered by forcing interactions between dominant and submissive dogs or redistributing toys, beds, or snacks to suit human interpretations of fairness. Regularly reprimanding an alpha dog for dominant behavior or ignoring one dog in favor of the other can create hostilities. Human meddling such as this can actually encourage the aggression of a dominant dog. The alpha dog will constantly feel a need to emphasize her status, which can escalate from a warning to unprovoked attacks on a weaker, lower-ranking dog.

These incidents may or may not take place in the owner's presence. Either way, the dogs will rapidly learn that the rules vary when the owner is or is not present. This undermines pack structure and creates a cycle of growing conflict.

Access to food, toys, and furniture are major sources of conflict. If the dogs exhibit any sort of dominance issues, it is best to feed them separately in crates, keep them all off the furniture, and make sure food and toys are not freely accessible to provoke battles. If the situation has already escalated to outright fighting, separating them is the only solution. Allowing the dogs to resolve their differences on their own is a really bad idea. Subsequent peace negotiations must be fully supervised.

Separation Anxiety

Separation anxiety is a trendy explanation for many bad habits. In fact, no puppy enjoys spending time alone. That does not imply that a puppy is incapable of learning how to cope in your absence. Teaching her to spend time alone should be a part of her daily routine as soon as you bring her home.

If you have neglected this crucial aspect of training, it is still possible to resolve this problem, but it is a much more involved training process. The puppy already has definite opinions about being alone and has probably devised a multitude of

Common Reasons for Dog Aggression

DOG AGGRESSION CAN BE TRIGGERED BY DOMINANCE, FEAR, *territorial behavior, or predation. It is not only dangerous for the dogs; humans can be seriously injured trying to break up a dogfight.*

- *A dominant puppy may begin asserting her authority by appropriating an older dog's food, toys, or bed, eventually provoking a confrontation.*
- *A puppy can develop a fear of other dogs if she is not well socialized with dogs. If she has poor "canine communication skills," she may become shy or defensive whenever she is approached by another dog.*
- *A naturally territorial dog may not hesitate to attack any strange dog she perceives as an intruder.*
- *Unless they have been properly socialized to smaller dogs as puppies, large predatory breeds may regard a small dog as prey.*

coping mechanisms. These may include constant howling and barking or devastation of the house. You won't like the latter, and your neighbors definitely won't like the former. To deal with the problem, you may need to start by putting the puppy in a separate room or a crate for just a few minutes each day. This duration can be gradually increased, but it may require several months of retraining (see chapter 8).

Attempts to revise bad habits through negative reinforcement (punishment) primarily teach the puppy that it is safer to wait until you leave to start howling and barking. Dealing with the problem may require professional help. When seeking advice for a behavior problem, don't neglect to research a trainer's background. Most dog trainers are professionally certified but

A rottweiler lounges on the couch, polishing off a shoe. This kind of destructive behavior may be a sign of separation anxiety.

credentials are worthless unless they are supplemented with substantial experience. Make sure the trainer has worked with your breed and *successfully* treated similar behavior problems.

Juvenile Delinquency

Adolescence represents a multifaceted extravaganza of stress, and all puppies are vulnerable to developing bad habits or behavioral problems during periods of social stress. Provide a positive outlet for your puppy's mental and physical energy, or brace yourself for the consequences. You may wake up one day and discover that a canine juvenile delinquent has set up shop in your living room.

There are warning signs and definite reasons a puppy turns into a juvenile delinquent, although it can be hard to spot the subtle but perilous shifts in behavior. You may be so focused on protecting and encouraging your puppy that her not-so-nice intentions are overlooked. Or your response to the puppy's behavior may unintentionally encourage a budding problem. For instance, you might not immediately notice your puppy's outgoing confident demeanor has burgeoned into dominant aggression and she has become the bully of the dog park. Each time she successfully intimidates another dog, she steps up these tactics. One day, she will pick on the wrong dog, and an outright dogfight will erupt. At that point, you'll realize that something is wrong. This doesn't mean that the puppy is inherently aggressive; she simply became more confident in her bad behavior after repeatedly getting away with it.

Don't place undue faith in temperament tests. These are simply behavior analyses and do not guarantee that your puppy

Obedience Training

ALTHOUGH IT'S FUN TO TRAIN YOUR PUPPY AT HOME, A **structured class has many benefits. A professional trainer can advise you on which methods will be most effective with your particular puppy. After she has mastered the basics of the sit, down, stay, and come commands, you may want to enroll her in a more advanced class or try for an obedience title. Obedience titles are offered by the AKC and UKC. They range from Companion Dog (CD), for dogs who earn three qualifying scores in basic obedience competitions, to Utility Dog Excellent (UDX), for dogs with ten qualifying scores in advanced level competitions. A new feature of obedience competition is the rally event, which is faster paced and less formal than the traditional obedience competition. In 2005, the AKC began awarding three levels of rally awards: novice, advanced, and excellent.**

Like this young owner, spend time with your puppy, pay attention to her interactions, and make sure she gets proper training and plenty of exercise.

A young husky enjoys an afternoon romp in a country field. Keeping a juvenile dog busy and well exercised can head off behavioral problems.

will automatically grow into a well-behaved dog. She will not simply outgrow a bad habit.

Keeping your puppy active is a great way to keep her out of trouble. Professional training classes are helpful in teaching her obedience and self-control. Regular exercise is another way for her to expend energy. Taking trips to dog-friendly parks and beaches and participating in dog sports are great outlets for her excess energy. A dog walking service or doggy day care can also help fill her daytime hours.

8

Puppy Training

An Australian shepherd receives a tasty treat for a good leash-training performance.

W E WANT OUR PUPPIES TO HAVE FUN AND ENJOY LIFE, which makes us hesitate to curb their irrepressible exuberance and unpredictable antics. Yet most of us have a hard time appreciating the charm of someone else's unruly children. The truth is that everyone, including you, will have a much greater appreciation for your puppy if you train him.

Don't put this off, thinking that your puppy is too immature. Most breeders start training their puppies when the dogs are just five or six weeks old. Don't make the mistake either of assuming that small breeds don't need training. Without basic good manners, even a tiny Chihuahua is capable of industrial strength barking, biting, or home destruction. For large breeds, an early start is essential. Otherwise, you will face the daunting prospect of training a boisterous teenage puppy weighing 50 to 100 pounds. For naturally dominant puppies, early consistent training reinforces their role in your pack, making them less likely to challenge your authority later on.

If you are raising a watchdog, early training is important to guide his instincts. His protective nature combined with a lack of proper training could condition him to bark at everyone and everything that encroaches on his territory. This is both ineffective and dangerous.

Be warned: your puppy is going to become trained regardless of whether you participate in the process. He will devise his own rules if you don't. His rules will likely include food stealing, barking at the neighbors, sleeping on the couch, jumping on guests, and excavating the backyard.

Basic training represents the bare essentials a puppy needs to learn, such as crate-training, house-training, riding in the car, and walking on the leash. Don't assume your puppy will under-

A border collie drives a group of sheep over a field. Developed as herders, border collies have a strong instinct to herd that isn't easily curbed.

stand these unless you teach him. Although training can modify strong personality traits, it will not completely change them. Some of your puppy's behavior is genetically predetermined, and certain instinctive behaviors will remain more or less evident. Instincts such as hunting, herding, and guarding emerge automatically as a puppy matures. Don't assume your pup is stubborn or contrary if he doesn't respond to your training methods by instantly overriding his genetic programming. You may just need to try a different approach.

Beginning Training

For a young puppy, short, frequent training sessions are best. Two or three minutes, whenever a good opportunity arises, will keep his interest and enthusiasm high. A structured training routine is not important at this age, but it is important to work in an area free of distractions. Concentration and focus are difficult for a puppy. This is one reason training classes, filled with other people and dogs, can be overwhelming.

Training must take place within a positive atmosphere. Regardless of his desire to please, your puppy will be incapable of learning anything unless he feels safe. Training will backfire if it becomes inadvertently associated with your impatience or anger.

Good or bad, habits are reinforced through a combination of instinct, memory, learning, and environment. Memory retention is largely dependent on the survival value of the information. Puppies can and do learn many things after a single experience. This includes things such as recognizing dangers and food sources. Complex learned behaviors such as house-training are less critical to survival and thus more difficult to retain in long-term memory.

Memory retention is also influenced by individual sensory abilities. Dogs are primarily designed to retain olfactory memories and those connected with social messages—because these are most likely to contribute to canine survival. This also varies by breed. Sensory ability and emotional thresholds are subject to genetic variation. For instance, some breeds are naturally more attuned to social rewards (praise and petting) and others are more likely to go gaga for a squeaky toy. Some are more visually oriented, and hand signals are an important part of training. Others are more likely to respond to vocal cues. This is why training methods and forms of reward don't work equally well for all puppies. However, it is much easier to strengthen any behavior pattern if the response and the reinforcing factors stem from the same motivation—especially if that motivation is rooted in a physical need, such as food.

Corrections

Puppies are puppies. They cannot be held to adult behavior standards. Be patient. However, you must be prepared to impose corrections if you expect your puppy to learn the rules. You do him no favor by avoiding discipline. Correction will not end his desire to bond with you. The idea of obeying a higher-ranking pack member is one of the first things a puppy learns from his mother. If you don't feel comfortable about reprimanding a puppy, do not choose a breed that may require frequent, firm corrections.

The amount and intensity of correction that's needed varies by breed, age, and individual temperament. Roughness or harsh corrections will be disastrous for a highly sensitive breed. The Chinese crested, for instance, is highly touch and sound sensitive and keenly affected by perceived social disapproval from an owner. Corrections must also be age appropriate. Don't assume that a young puppy "knows better" when he does something wrong. Puppies need time to learn and remember rules about things such as house-training and chewing.

Select a word such as *bad* or *no* and be prepared to present it in a no-nonsense fashion. Volume is not important; what dogs do understand is the message of low vocal tones. Look the puppy right in the eye and be firm. A weak reprimand is worthless; the puppy may simply ignore you and eventually decide that your corrections mean nothing. If he refuses to comply, you will need to step up the intensity of your corrections until he does. Backing down or ignoring bad behavior only makes matters worse in the long run.

By taking the time to instill the idea that "*no* means *no*," you will not need to resort to more forceful correction methods later. This does not require teaching the puppy to fear you. Done right, it should accomplish exactly the opposite.

- Corrections must always be done when the behavior occurs—never afterward.
- Say it as if you mean it, no hesitating or wheedling—do it once and do it right.
- Never let the puppy ignore your correction.
- Don't overdo it. Reserve the word of correction for immediately stopping bad behavior.
- Always praise the puppy after he obeys.
- Maintain emotional self-control; if you feel as if you are going to lose your temper, put the puppy outside or in his crate until you cool down.

Rewards

Successful or otherwise, training sessions should always be followed up with a reward.

By praising the puppy after he obeys, you reinforce both the correction and the idea that compliance is the best way to

For learning his lessons, a Pomeranian pup gets a delicious biscuit. Be sure the proffered treat isn't too big for the dog, however.

keep peace. It is crucial that the puppy understand that once the undesirable behavior has stopped, he is immediately back in your good graces.

Crate-Training

Crate-training your puppy is valuable for several reasons. Most of all, the crate will ensure that he is safe when you cannot supervise him. It also greatly simplifies the house-training process. With a proper introduction, your puppy will have no problem learning to accept the crate. He will come to regard it as his own safe retreat, something we all need from time to time.

Most puppies instinctively seek the security of a den and do not hesitate to enter a crate. Normally, they feel safe in a crate and will pile in there to sleep together. It satisfies their social and territorial instincts. Puppies who are first introduced to a crate along with their "pack" of littermates usually have no trouble adjusting to it later on.

The puppy should feel comfortable about entering and leaving the crate. Do not force him into the crate; teach him to enter and exit. This way, you will not be faced with the problem of a puppy who must be pried out of the crate or shoots out of the door like a cannonball.

Use a special word to ask the puppy to go into the crate. Give him a treat when he complies. It's sometimes helpful to hide a treat in the back of the crate. Do the same when you want him to come out: open the door, give the signal, and reward the desired response. A calm, well-behaved exit from the crate should be rewarded. If the puppy refuses to come out, try to coax him. If that doesn't work, physically pick him up and lift him out of the crate. Don't make a big fuss about it but don't let him think it is OK to ignore your wishes. If the puppy has a habit of wildly flying out as soon as the crate door opens, don't praise this behavior. Tell the puppy to sit quietly and pay no attention to him until he does so. When he obeys, praise his response but don't get him too keyed up, or you will have to start all over again. Lavish praise tends to be counterproductive for crate-training because the puppy easily misinterprets this attention. Praise tends to get him too wound up and reinforces the desire to be out of the crate.

Do not allow the puppy to get into the habit of defending the crate and refusing to come out when called. Never allow him

A golden retriever sits contentedly in his crate. Early training will help your dog accept the crate.

to deny you access or prevent you from removing something from it. A favorite puppy game is to gather up all the toys and proceed to guard this stash against all comers. This can escalate into territorial aggression if you do not intervene.

The crate should be furnished with a blanket and a few toys. Don't leave a water dish in the crate for training sessions unless you want to clean up the mess. To begin with, leave the puppy in the crate for just a minute or two. Gradually increase the time over several days. When it is time to let the puppy out, do it in a calm, neutral manner.

The puppy may initially whine, cry, or dig, but he will soon fall asleep or occupy himself with a toy if he does not get any reaction from you. This is precisely how a mother dog responds to a puppy's inappropriate whining; she ignores it. If you keep going over to check, talking to the puppy, putting different toys in the crate, or sitting next to the crate trying to sooth the puppy, he will never cease this behavior—you are simply reinforcing the bad habit. Very young puppies should be confined only for short periods of time to travel, eat, or nap. If they feel frightened, trapped, or isolated in the crate, they will associate the crate with punishment. They also need to relieve themselves frequently, and excessive crate confinement will completely undermine house-training. If a puppy gets into the habit of eliminating in his crate, it is very difficult to discourage. In general, crate confinement can be safely increased by one hour each month until the puppy has sufficient bladder control to make it through the night.

The puppy must also become accustomed to the idea that the crate can move. Initially, most dogs find this feeling unsettling and can become agitated, especially during car trips. Gradual introduction helps to alleviate anxiety and lessen bad reactions such as travel sickness.

House-Training

Although many puppies are sent to their new homes with an assurance that they are reliably house-trained, this holds true only for familiar territory. A puppy cannot generalize about house-training rules. He must learn to transfer the rules to his new home.

When a puppy enters a new home, existing patterns can either be reinforced or undermined. To make this transition without a lapse in house-training, be vigilant, and consistently provide positive reinforcement for desired behavior. Do not make the mistake of assuming that the puppy is house-trained after a few successful experiences. This only means that your message is getting across; it does not mean that a reliable behavior pattern has been established. This takes time.

Puppy Instincts

House-training is a perfect example of a natural instinct that can be easily reinforced. As soon as he is able to walk, a puppy tries to eliminate away from his den, where he eats or sleeps. This instinct surfaces when a puppy is just four or five weeks old and will have a lifelong impact on elimination habits.

Although a puppy knows that he should leave his nest to eliminate, he has no instinctive desire to apply this fastidious behavior to territory beyond his immediate eating and sleeping area. In this respect, instinct is quite the opposite. Elimination is a means of defining territory. This is why locations with a strong social importance, such the living room furniture, usually become favorite targets of poorly house-trained dogs. Instinct will direct a puppy's behavior unless you instill a more rewarding alternative through consistent training.

Methods and Routines

Puppies can be reliably trained to follow any house-training routine that you choose. Indoor dogs can learn to eliminate on newspaper or wee-wee pads or in litter boxes. They can be trained to faithfully go out a dog door and do their business in one spot in the yard. They can be trained to relieve themselves on command during walks. However you choose to house-train your puppy, it is crucial to accustom him to the routine from a

An owner teaches her bichon frise to use newspapers in a kitchen corner. Early and consistent training are needed when house-training a new dog.

young age and reward consistently for the desired behavior. After four months of age, dogs become increasingly reluctant to revise these patterns.

Settle on one strategy before you bring the puppy home. Begin as soon as he arrives, and do not deviate from the plan. Some puppies can be house-trained within a few days; others can take quite a bit longer. Don't be tempted to experiment with training methods if you don't get immediate results.

Learning the Puppy's Cues

Young puppies can learn to conform to a house-training schedule, but they cannot be expected to let you know when they need to go out. Sometimes they will, and sometimes they won't.

Don't depend on this when deciding that it is time to put the puppy outside or on his paper. Once you become familiar with his habits, you can pretty well predict when he needs to go out. Circling, sniffing, and squatting are reliable clues.

When your puppy feels the need to go, don't complicate the situation by expecting him to navigate his way around the house to find the right spot in time. During the house-training period, you are not doing the puppy any favors by allowing him to roam freely around the house or a large yard. If you want the puppy to use a designated area of the yard, fence off the rest. The scent of urine will reinforce his desire to use that spot.

Schedules

Puppies need to go as soon as they wake up in the morning, immediately after breakfast, and after a play session. In the afternoon, they'll need to go after lunch, several times during late-day playtime, and again after a nap. In the evening, elimination usually occurs after their dinner and once more before bedtime.

Puppies usually learn to control their elimination during the night at a fairly young age. Do your best to encourage this, but don't expect miracles. There will be times when you must get up and take your puppy out during the night. If he regularly needs to relieve himself in the middle of the night, try feeding a half hour earlier and restricting water intake for an hour or two before bedtime. It also helps to make sure the puppy is good and tired by bedtime. This means evening walks and play sessions. Under no circumstances should you get into the habit of waking up and asking the puppy if he wants to go out. Trust me, he will, and your actions will reinforce the habit.

A weimaraner sits among some plants in the backyard. If you want your dog to use only certain spots in the yard when eliminating, start training him immediately.

The Training Process

When you take the puppy to his elimination spot, do not distract him with praise or treats before he has had time to do his business. Take him to the spot and ignore him. Otherwise, he will become more interested in playing with you—especially after he realizes that you have a reward. Even if he needs to go, do not expect this to happen immediately. Give the puppy at least fifteen to twenty minutes before giving up. One of the most common house-training mistakes is taking the puppy back into the house and turning him loose, assuming that he really did not need to go. Instead, put the puppy in his crate, wait fifteen to thirty minutes, and try again. You may need to do this two or three times before you get results.

A Brittany receives a tasty morsel for a job well done. Constant, positive feedback with treats is essential when you're house-training a dog.

House-training takes a variable amount of time, but positive reinforcement is one thing that can speed up the process. Every time the puppy does the right thing in the right place, positive feedback must be immediate. Dogs are very good at making connections between their actions and rewards. Verbal rewards are good, but food rewards have an even stronger effect. Reinforcing this natural instinct is far easier than correcting house-training problems later on.

House-training can be frustrating, but it is pointless to scold a puppy after the fact or reprimand him when he is caught in the act. A puppy cannot make the desired association between crime and punishment. He has no ulterior motives for eliminating in inappropriate spots. After the deed is done, the puppy will have no thoughts on the matter whatsoever. Reprimanding or punishing a puppy after the fact is an excellent way to turn a temporary training problem into a phobia or a chronic attention-seeking strategy.

Yelling at the puppy or grabbing him and running out the door when he has an accident will definitely frighten him. He may simply decide that it's never safe to eliminate anytime, anywhere in your presence. Toy breeds are especially good at mastering the "fast and sneaky" approach. After a puppy adopts this strategy, house-training becomes far more challenging. Many transgressions are small enough to go unnoticed until much later.

Accidents are apt to occur, and you must be prepared to cope with this in a neutral, detached way if you choose to have a puppy. Consistent negative reactions from you can cause secondary behavior problems. You may find yourself dealing with training problems far more complicated than house-training, such as fearfulness or aggression.

House-Training Regressions

There are many reasons why a reliably house-trained puppy can experience a relapse.

- Major changes in the puppy's usual routine: If the puppy is accustomed to eliminating only when out for a walk, in his own backyard, or on newspaper, it will take some time to revise this pattern.

- Fear and anxiety: Make sure that the puppy is not being intimidated or frightened when he does go out. This can come from another dominant dog at home, neighborhood dogs, humans, or something unexpected in his environment such as a noisy construction crew next door.

- Separation anxiety: If house-training accidents occur only in your absence, the behavior may be a result of separation anxiety. This can be caused by major changes in the puppy's environment, excessive attachment to one family member, or neglect.

- Physical causes: Accidents can also be caused by something as simple as too many treats or a change in diet. Or it may be more complicated, such as intestinal parasites or a bladder infection, which may require medical treatment from your veterinarian.

It is not unusual for a well-trained puppy to have accidents during adolescence. Both males and females can begin territorial marking around five or six months of age. In some cases, training pants or bellybands can help to discourage this habit. These products, available for males and females of any size, work as a diaper of sorts to prevent the dog from marking any territory. The unpleasant sensation of urinating while wearing one of these garments can be an effective deterrent.

Common Bad Habits

Most juvenile misbehavior is the result of communication failure. Without proper training, your puppy will make his own rules. In many cases, owners don't recognize how significant an issue a bad habit is until the puppy has gotten big enough to cause a lot of inconvenience. By that point, remedial training is the only solution. Common bad habits that puppies form at a young age include the following.

Failing to Come When Called

A puppy effortlessly learns his name because this word is immediately connected to rewards. For most puppies, coming when called is spontaneous, unless something happens to revise that. Don't complicate matters. Reinforce his natural inclination to come to you by keeping things positive. When you call the puppy and he obeys, always offer praise and treats. Don't make the mistake of assuming that the puppy has learned this lesson after a few successful responses. It must be constantly reinforced throughout training. If your puppy happens to ignore your command to come, which is bound to happen sometime during training, don't let him get away with it. Get the puppy's attention and encourage him until he obeys. Don't try to accomplish this through negative reinforcement such as by saying "no" or "bad dog." Encourage the puppy with a treat or toy, and praise him when he finally obeys. Even if he repeatedly ignored you, once he has come, he must be rewarded for doing so; saying "no" or "bad" reinforces the idea that coming when called will be punished. The puppy must never learn to associate coming to you with possible punishment.

Nipping and Biting

A puppy learns not to bite when playing with his mother. With a growl or snap, she teaches her puppies at a very young age how hard is too hard to bite. Transferring this lesson to interactions with humans is not automatic. That part of the lesson is your job. The only way to do it is to play with your puppy and provide an impressive reaction when he nips. It does not matter whether the nip is intentional or accidental or whether it is actually painful.

Don't expect this to sink in immediately. For some puppies, it takes months of continuous practice. Refusing to play with the puppy is counterproductive. He will never learn to understand these rules. Your puppy needs five to ten minutes of interactive play each day to learn bite inhibition.

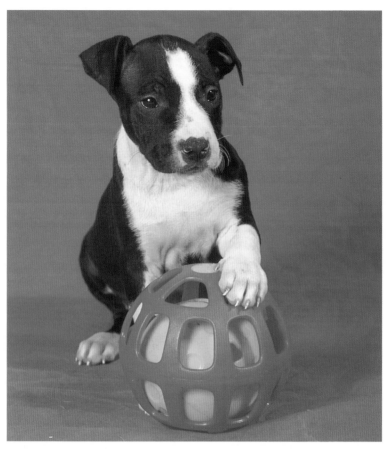

Paw resting possessively on a toy ball, an American Staffordshire terrier guards his property. You must teach your puppy to surrender at your command any object he is eating or guarding.

Guarding Valuables

Your puppy must learn to surrender on command anything he is eating, holding, or guarding. This may be a toy, a treat, or something he should definitely not have in his mouth, such as your shoe. For some breeds, collecting and guarding objects is an overriding instinct, and early training is crucial to discourage possessiveness. When the puppy is guarding or holding something that you want, put your hand on it, say "drop it," and offer a treat. If the item happens to be clenched in his jaws, he will have no choice but to open his mouth and drop it to get the treat. Be calm, but firm. If the puppy refuses, physically remove the item from his mouth. Follow this up with praise and a treat. Never follow releasing the object with punishment, but don't take no for an answer. Discourage any snarling or growling with an emphatic "no!"

Refusing to Be Picked Up

A puppy's earliest contact with humans is being picked up, held, and carried. Some naturally accept this, and others perceive it as dangerous. Don't assume that a puppy will be relaxed about it. He may panic and struggle when lifted or restrained. Training can make a life or death difference for a seriously injured pet. For large, strong dogs, it can be impossible to get a grip if they are uncooperative. Small dogs can be seriously injured if dropped when struggling to get loose.

If your puppy is nervous when picked up, this must be addressed while he is still small and easy to handle. Your size and ability to overpower your puppy may intensify his fear. Pick him up frequently, and reward him with praise and treats for cooperation. At first, you may hold him for only a few seconds at a time, so it must be done many times each day. If the puppy becomes agitated, put him down. Don't hold on to a struggling puppy and attempt to soothe him. As he struggles and realizes he can't get away, his adrenaline level and anxiety rise. Praising this reaction, which is what you are doing by attempting to soothe the puppy, will reinforce the idea that this fearful response is proper. Put the puppy down, and ignore him until he is calm. Then call him to you, and assure him that everything is all right.

Objecting to Grooming

A dog's uncooperative attitude is one of the major reasons owners neglect basic grooming. Nail trimming and teeth cleaning are usually the biggest problems. Even if your puppy does not yet need it, go through the motions of these chores at least two to three minutes every day. Be firm and consistent. The puppy must learn that he's required to tolerate grooming on your terms. That means no growling, no barking, no wiggling, and no squirming. Remember to reward cooperation.

After allowing herself to being picked up, a dalmatian pup sits quietly in her owner's hands. Pick up and reward your puppy frequently to overcome any fears of being handled.

Good sized but soft, this toy provides a West Highland white terrier pup with something to chew on—other than a piece of your furniture.

Destructive Chewing

Chewing is not a temporary phase. Resign yourself to the idea that your puppy is going to chew. The trick is to make sure this is directed toward something appropriate. (See chapter 4, puppy proofing your home.) It is your job to keep the valuables out of reach and provide sufficiently enticing alternatives. Big puppies need sturdy and challenging chew toys. They will immediately chomp small or flimsy objects to pieces and choke on the debris. Tiny puppies need something that will yield satisfying results from their destructive efforts. Otherwise, they will lose interest and set their sights on the kitchen chairs.

Supervision, rather than correction, is the only way to curb inappropriate chewing. When the puppy begins to chew something inappropriate, say "no," take the item away, and offer an alternative. A young puppy has a short attention span. Don't assume that this message will immediately sink in. The puppy may happily gnaw on his bone for fifteen minutes, then revert to the arm of the couch. Supervision is essential until the puppy is old enough to understand and remember the idea.

Dog destruction is part of the package when you have a puppy. Inevitably, you will discover that the puppy has chewed something valuable. Take it in stride. The puppy is incapable of making any connection between crime and punishment. The incident may help reinforce your own training to supervise adequately and keep valuables out of reach.

Jumping Up

Enthusiasm is self-reinforcing. If you act excited, the puppy becomes excited, and his adrenaline level rises—he becomes more excited and soon his actions are out of control. Wild behavior in the house—including jumping on people or furniture—should never be substituted for regular exercise. Even if your puppy is too small to do damage, he can be injured jumping off a chair or charging down the stairs in wild abandon. Puppies do not possess good coordination or adult muscle or bone strength.

Rather than trying to stop it later, don't encourage overexcited behavior to start with. Don't chase the puppy around the house if he goes into a play frenzy. Don't respond. Ignore him until he comes to you and obeys your command to sit quietly. Be firm but calm. Reward self-control and ignore overreaction.

A rottweiler obediently lies in the *down* position. Teach your dog basic commands such as *down* right away to help control his behavior.

Everyone who interacts with the puppy must reinforce this message. If one person continues to reward jumping, the habit will persist.

Puppies don't have much self-control, but this will improve with time and practice. Teaching basic commands like *sit* and *down* helps. As long as he knows that a reward is forthcoming, his energy and enthusiasm can be channeled into any direction that you choose.

Barking and Whining

Dogs long ago figured out that the squeaky wheel gets the grease. Barking not only draws attention but also relieves boredom. Within a canine pack, unwarranted crying and whining is ignored, which encourages a puppy to stop. But barking can be easily reinforced if it gets a positive response from humans. Distressed puppies broadcast anxiety through whining. Many things can trigger it, not all of them requiring attention. Dogs use it, for instance, to deflect confrontations, to express frustration, and to wheedle a taste of your dinner. Normally, whining decreases as a puppy matures, unless you make a habit of encouraging it.

Puppies usually start territorial defensive barking around three to four months of age. Some breeds are more prone to this behavior, but most puppies have the potential for it. If it is ignored or rewarded, barking at the mailman can escalate into defensive aggression.

The first step in teaching the puppy to be quiet is actually to teach the puppy to bark. Do something that usually prompts him to bark, such as knocking on the door. When he complies, give the command *speak* or *bark* and reward. Clicker training (discussed later in this chapter) works well for teaching both commands. The puppy will make this connection in short order because he is being rewarded for something he enjoys. Once the puppy understands *speak*, work on *quiet*. This usually takes longer. Once the puppy is barking, give the command to be quiet. The puppy may ignore you, but he cannot bark forever. Showing him a treat will get his attention. If nothing else, it is impossible to eat and bark simultaneously. When he finally shuts up, repeat the command and give the reward.

Many owners encourage excess barking without realizing it. If your puppy barks to demand something such as food or a walk, don't comply until he obeys your request to be quiet. Never let a barking puppy out of his crate or encourage a noisy welcome home.

Leash Training

Leash training is a combination of several new experiences: learning the feel of the collar and the restraint of the leash, and walking with a person. Walking on the leash in a public place is an additional lesson in socialization. Combining all these ideas at once may be too much for a young puppy to assimilate.

Present them gradually and systematically. Let the puppy get used to the collar for a day or two before progressing to the leash. Most puppies will ignore the collar if they are preoccupied with chew toys or dinner. Older puppies may take much longer to accept wearing a collar.

Initial leash training should take place somewhere free of distractions. Puppies are not very coordinated and need practice to figure out how to walk without getting the lead tangled around their legs or yours. This also requires patience and concentration on your part. Five minutes a day for a week is plenty. Walking in public places is an important part of socialization, but don't start this until he feels comfortable with the leash and collar.

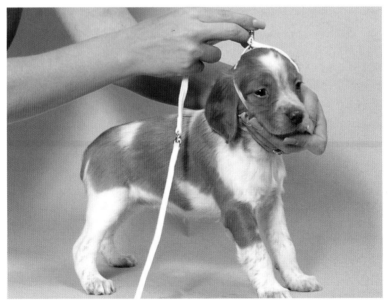

Leash training lessons begin for a Brittany spaniel. The first step is getting the puppy used to the collar.

Some puppies never object to the leash; others refuse to budge as soon as they feel the slightest pressure or may resort to a tantrum. Be patient, and try to coax the puppy along with a toy or treat. Never pull or drag him. As part of your pack, your puppy wants to follow you—as long as you don't do anything to discourage the idea, such as acting impatient or being too forceful. Always react in a positive manner no matter how frustrating leash training may become. It may help to take the puppy out with a dog who is already leash trained. Nothing encourages a better attitude about the leash and collar than regular walks to the park.

Clicker Training

Clicker training has become popular for many types of dog training because it is such an easy way to instill a positive connection between a puppy's action and a reward. The premise is very simple: puppies are very good at making connections between actions and immediate rewards, and they quickly learn that the sound of the clicker signals an imminent treat. You will need a good supply of bite-size treats. Clicker training works best if the puppy does not need time to chew and swallow after every click-and-treat sequence. Cheerios, cheese bits, or chopped hot dogs work well. Clickers are sold in most pet supply stores.

Start by simply clicking the clicker and giving the puppy a reward. Do this ten to twenty times a day for a couple of days. Vary the location of the training, and have different people practice with the puppy. Otherwise, he may not be forming the correct association with the sound of the click and the treat—this is important as training progresses, as the click will be followed by an actual command, then the treat for obedience. As soon as the puppy understands that a click

This rottweiler waits in the sit position for his owner's next command. You can teach commands such as *sit* with the clicker training method.

means a reward, you can employ this method to simplify many different kinds of training.

Clicker training is an easy way to teach the *sit* and *down* commands. Don't force the puppy into position. Just wait until he does so on his own. When your puppy is sitting, give the *sit* command, then click and reward. The faster you produce the treat, the better. Very quickly, the puppy will learn that sitting, the word *sit*, and the click signal a treat. After a few successful responses, try giving the command and click and waiting for the puppy to sit before offering the treat. Ignore inappropriate responses, and reward correct ones. Use exactly the same procedure for *down*.

After the puppy understands *sit* and *down*, you can proceed to *stay*. Using your click-and-treat method, have the puppy sit or lie down. Immediately follow this with the new command, *stay*. Wait a few seconds before giving the treat. If the puppy gets up and moves, withhold the treat and start over. The critical thing is to give the reward while the puppy is still stationary, even if he is so only for a second. Otherwise, he will not associate the appropriate action and the reward. Once the puppy gets the idea, gradually increase the number of seconds that he must stay still, moving a few inches farther away from him each time. This requires patience and repetition, as you are also improving the puppy's naturally short attention span. Even if he seems to be catching on, for safety always practice with the puppy on lead or in a fenced area.

Puppy Training Classes

In addition to teaching basic obedience training, classes provide opportunities for puppies to practice their social skills with both humans and other dogs. Training classes can be a perfect opportunity to meet age-appropriate canine playmates. In addition, no matter how much time you devote to training and socializing your puppy at home, problems are going to arise. An experienced dog trainer can provide you with priceless advice on issues of behavior modification.

Don't wait until your puppy develops bad habits before joining a training class. Enroll your puppy in class at about twelve weeks of age. There is no clear timeline concerning when spontaneous socialization wanes. It is highly individual, depending on environment and genetics. For most puppies, it happens gradually between eleven and fourteen weeks, so take advantage of his curiosity while you can. By this age, contact with other dogs should no longer pose a health risk, and it will be highly beneficial to your puppy's social development.

A puppy kindergarten class should be your first choice. These classes are specifically structured to accommodate puppies' limited attention spans and minimize the intimidation factor that may occur in classes that include older (bigger) dogs. At the same time, the class should provide more than entertainment and social approval. It should offer ways to enhance your puppy's learning potential and offset behavior problems. The instructor should offer guidance to help puppies develop appropriate social skills, especially those needed to interact with people.

Limited participation in a regular training class can still provide positive interaction with new people and dogs of all shapes and sizes. Regardless of the size or nature of the class, the instructor should maintain a controlled environment. If your puppy becomes frightened or intimidated, the experience can do more harm than good. Under the best of circumstances, there is a chance that puppies will become bored or nervous. Bring along a few toys and treats to offset any initial apprehension. If the puppy can be convinced to eat or play, this is a good indication that he feels comfortable. After two or three classes, most puppies are keen to return and clearly enjoy the experience.

A Final Note

You may be reading this book in contemplation of getting a puppy. Or you may have already taken that big step. Either way, this book will provide you with a clear understanding of the commitment involved in raising, training, and caring for a puppy. No book can adequately describe the joy that a puppy will bring to your life.

Appendix

Dog Registries

AMERICAN KENNEL CLUB
5580 Centerview Drive
Raleigh, NC 27606
(919) 233-9767
E-mail: info@akc.org
http://www.akc.org

AMERICAN MIXED BREED OBEDIENCE REGISTRY
179 Niblick Road #113
Paso Robles, CA 93446
(805) 226-9275
http://www.amborusa.org

UNITED KENNEL CLUB
100 E. Kilgore Road
Kalamazoo, MI 49002
(269) 343-9020
E-mail: pbkckell@ukcdogs.com
http://www.ukcdogs.com

Helpful Organizations

THE AMERICAN ANIMAL HOSPITAL ASSOCIATION
12575 West Bayaud Avenue
Lakewood, CO 80228
(303) 986-2800
E-mail: info@aahanet.org
http://www.aahanet.org

AMERICAN VETERINARY MEDICAL ASSOCIATION
1931 North Meacham Road, Suite 100
Schaumburg, IL, 60173
(847) 925-8070
E-mail: avmainfo@avma.org
http://www.avma.org

ASSOCIATION OF PET DOG TRAINERS
5096 Sand Road SE
Iowa City, IA 52240
(800) PET-DOGS
E-mail: information@apdt.com
http://www.apdt.com

CERTIFICATION COUNCIL FOR PET DOG TRAINERS
1350 Broadway, 17th floor
New York, NY 10018
(212) 356-0682
E-mail: joan@ccpdt.org
http://www.ccpdt.org

NORTH AMERICAN DOG AGILITY COUNCIL
115 South Highway 3
Cataldo, ID 83810
http://www.nadac.com

ORTHOPEDIC FOUNDATION FOR ANIMALS
2300 E. Nifong Boulevard
Colombia, MO 65201
(573) 442-0418
E-mail: ofa@offa.org
http://www.offa.org

THERAPY DOGS INTERNATIONAL
88 Bartley Square
Flanders, NJ 07836
(973) 252-9800
E-mail: tdi@gti.net
http://www.tdi-dog.org

Online Resources

Online resources to find information on a variety of subjects

ADOPTION
http://www.petfinder.org

AVMA POISON GUIDE
http://www.avma.org/pubhlth/poisgde.asp#acet

GENERAL INFORMATION
http://www.animalnetwork.com
http://www.dogchannel.com

HEALTH CARE
http://www.ani-med.com
http://www.healthypet.com
http://www.merckvetmanual.com

INFORMATION ON BREEDERS
http://www.nopuppymills.com

NUTRITION
http://www.aafco.org
http://www.petfoodinstitute.org

TRAINING AND BEHAVIOR
http://www.apdt.com
http://www.dogforum.info

Glossary

AKC: American Kennel Club

AKC papers: papers issued by the American Kennel Club that certify a dog's individual registration number, breed, sex, color, registered name, breeder, owner, sire, and dam

alpha dog: highest-ranking dog in a pack, may be the largest, or oldest dog

bloat: condition in which gas or fluids trapped in the stomach causes distension of the stomach or the stomach's turning over or twisting, blocking the entrance and exit of the stomach; also known as torsion and gastric dilation

breed standard: official description of ideal features, faults, and disqualifications of a breed

canines: upper and lower pointed teeth next to the incisors (upper canines sometimes referred to as eyeteeth); also known as fangs

crossbred: a puppy whose sire and dam are two different breeds

dam: a female dog with a litter of puppies

deciduous teeth: small sharp teeth that emerge by eight weeks of age; replaced by permanent teeth by four to five months of age; also known as milk teeth or baby teeth

demodectic mange: skin disease caused by a microscopic parasitic mite that inhabits skin and hair follicles, causing crusty or bare patches, most often around the face; most common in short haired-breeds and puppies under twelve months of age dominant: higher-ranking individual in a pack

double coat: combination of protective outer coat and softer undercoat for insulation and weatherproofing

gait: manner in which puppy walks or runs

groom: bathe, brush, comb, and trim to clean and neaten a dog's coat

hackles: raised hairs on the back and neck; may be done in fear or anger

heat: female's seasonal breeding cycle, every six to eight months, characterized by bleeding and attraction to males; also known as season and estrus

hierarchy: the sequence of rank in a pack; the pecking order

hip dysplasia (CHD): hereditary malformation of the hip joints, causing arthritic changes; surgical correction required in severe cases

incisors: front teeth—six upper and six lower

interactive play: play with other individuals, either canine or human, to learn social skills

investigative play: early form of puppy play to learn about the environment

littermates: siblings born in same litter

monorchid: presence of only one testicle in the scrotum, with the second retained in the abdomen

neutering: surgical removal of both testicles to prevent reproduction

pack: social group that lives together in an established hierarchy pack status: an individual's ranking within a pack; can change due to social influences

pedigree: puppy's family tree, showing several generations of ancestors

positive reinforcement: providing positive inducements, such as praise or treats, to reward desired behavior in order to encourage habit formation

predatory drive: canine hunting instinct; most puppies exhibit one or more parts of typical hunting behavior

progressive retinal atrophy (PRA): hereditary condition causing progressive blindness

purebred: dog whose sire and dam are the same breed

random bred: dog whose ancestry may be estimated, based on a resemblance to certain breeds, but cannot be verified; also known as mixed breed, mongrel, or mutt

shock: acute circulatory failure, characterized by pallor of mucous membranes, low blood pressure, weak rapid pulse, low body temperature, and weak respiration

sighthound: dog who hunts by sight, such as greyhound or whippet

smooth coat: short, flat, dense hair, which may be single or double

socialization: introducing puppies to unusual aspects in their environment

spay: surgical removal of ovaries and uterus to prevent reproduction

submissive: lower-ranking individual in a pack

Index